**Library of Congress
Cataloging-in-Publication Data**

Shedd, Warner, 1934 –
    The Kids' wildlife book : exploring animal
worlds through indoor/outdoor crafts &
experiences / Warner Shedd.
        p.   cm.
        "A Williamson kids can! book."
        Includes index.
        ISBN 0-913589-77-2
        1. Animals—Juvenile literature.   2. Zoology
—Study and teaching—Activity programs—
Juvenile literature.   (1. Animals.)   I. Title.
        QL49.S482 1994   93-42958
        591—dc20   CIP
                                                    AC

Cover and interior design: Trezzo–Braren Studio
Illustrations: Loretta Trezzo Braren
Printing: Capital City Press

Williamson Publishing Co.
Box 185
Charlotte, Vermont 05445
(800) 234-8791

Manufactured in the United States of America

10 9 8 7 6 5 4 3 2

A Williamson *Kids Can!* Book

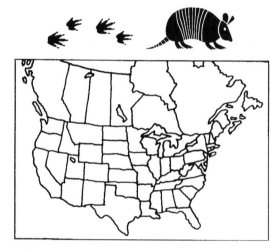

WILLIAMSON
KIDS CAN!

THE KIDS' WILDLIFE BOOK

by Warner Shedd

ILLUSTRATED BY LORETTA TREZZO BRAREN

WILLIAMSON PUBLISHING • CHARLOTTE, VERMONT 05445

DEDICATION: *For Julie and Davey*

ACKNOWLEDGEMENTS

Special thanks to my wife, Edie, our three children, Suzy, Mark, and David, and daughters-in-law Ellen and Peggy, for their constant interest and support throughout this project.

Many thanks also to Susan and Jack Williamson and their entire staff for making the publication of this book such an easy and enjoyable process.

Space doesn't permit me to list every source of information used in writing this book. However, a few people stand out as particularly deserving of mention:

Jim DiStefano, Ron Regan, and Cedric Alexander, specialists respectively in fur-bearing mammals, white-tailed deer, and moose with the Vermont Fish and Wildlife Department, for their immense patience in answering my seemingly endless stream of questions.

Chris Rimmer of the Vermont Institute of Natural Science and Chris Fichtel of the Vermont Nongame and Natural Heritage Program, for their expert assistance on birds; also Steve Perrin of the Nongame and Natural Heritage Program for his advice in locating many different sources of information about a variety of creatures;

Dr. Charles Jonkel, University of Montana at Missoula and head of the Ursid Research and Border Grizzly Project; Gary Alt, bear biologist with the Pennsylvania Game Commission; and Charles Willey, bear specialist with the Vermont Fish and Wildlife Department for their great knowledge of bears and insights into their behavior;

L. David Mech, U.S. Fish and Wildlife Service biologist, for his wonderful and accurate books on wolves, the result of many years of dedicated field research;

J. David Henry, whose research and superb writings and photographs concerning the red fox make him Mech's counterpart in the world of foxes;

Bat Conservation International for its vast store of knowledge about bats.

CONTENTS

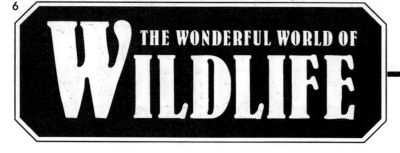

THE WONDERFUL WORLD OF WILDLIFE

Wildlife is quite simply — wonderful. It is fascinating and fun; it makes us curious to know more, and it makes us giggle, too. There are many reasons why almost everyone likes wildlife. For one thing, we can simply enjoy the great variety of different creatures — each with its own combination of size, shape, and color; necessary habitat; and its distinctive way of moving and interacting with the world around it. For another, each type of wildlife has its own way of gathering food, finding shelter from the weather, taking care of its young, and in some cases, staking out its territory.

Getting to know wildlife adds interest and pleasure to our own lives. Take a moment in every day — especially on a day when you are feeling a bit down or grumpy — and watch some wildlife out your window. Look at a squirrel leaping from limb to limb, watch a pigeon pecking for some food, or look at a bat swooping overhead gobbling up mosquitoes. Just watching wildlife can make us feel good.

Wildlife also reminds us that we share our planet Earth with a huge number of other creatures. Our health, as well as theirs, depends on how well we treat our planet and its natural resources.

The very *wildness* of wildlife also attracts us. House pets are wonderful, too, but there's something very special about animals that are wild and free — that don't depend on humans and still live as they have for thousands or even millions of years.

Habitat Is the Key

If we're going to continue to have lots of wildlife to enjoy, we have to be sure to preserve plenty of *habitat*. Habitat is the special place and conditions that each kind of wildlife needs in order to survive. It includes food, water, shelter, and enough space to move freely. Think of all of the different kinds of wildlife — mammals, amphibians, birds, reptiles, fish, and insects. Each has its own special habitat requirements.

Some types of habitat — called *critical habitat* — are so important that wildlife can't survive long without it. Nesting areas for birds and wintering areas for deer are good examples of critical habitat. We must respect and preserve good habitat — especially critical habitat — in order to have plenty of wildlife.

Keep Wild Things Wild

We must all understand that wild animals are just that — *wild!* They aren't pets, and they won't make good pets, no matter how cute they look. People often try to save orphaned baby animals by raising them as pets, but this is not a good idea.

Actually, many of these animals aren't orphans at all. Their mother may be watching from a hiding place, or she may just be off gathering food. Once they grow up, they can be very destructive. They don't react like cats and dogs, and they can "turn" on people very suddenly. Every year, for instance, people are badly injured or even killed by supposedly gentle "pet" deer, or badly bitten by animals like "pet" raccoons.

Another good reason not to try to make pets of wildlife is that it's strictly against the law in most states. One of the best reasons not to keep wild *mammals* (animals with fur) as pets is that it can be very dangerous. Have you ever heard of rabies? It's a deadly disease that mammals can get, and they can give it to humans because we're mammals, too. That's why you should NEVER handle, touch, pet, or pick up wild mammals. You should especially keep far away from any that act sick or mean!

So enjoy wild animals from afar, and leave them as they should be — free to live in the wild.

SAFETY GUIDE TO THE OUTDOORS

There's so much fun to be had in the great outdoors that sometimes we forget to always use SAFETY FIRST! How do you avoid getting hurt while you're out in the woods or fields enjoying wildlife and its habitat? Here are a few simple rules that will help you.

1. Never go near ponds, lakes, brooks, and rivers unless you have a grown-up with you. There are no exceptions to this rule. Please always obey it.

2. Never go into any big woods unless you have a grown-up with you to help you find the way out. It is easy to get lost in the woods.

3. Never touch or pick up any wild mammals, or try to feed them out of your hand. Don't try to bring them home as pets, either.

4. Be aware of the danger of the disease *rabies*, which humans can get from infected mammals. Here are some things you should do to prevent rabies.

★ Make sure your pets are vaccinated against rabies.

★ Don't try to touch any wild mammals. This is *especially* true if they act sick, mean, or strange in any way. If you see a wild mammal that behaves in an unusual way, stay far away from it and report it at once to a grown-up, who should call a conservation officer.

★ Don't touch the carcasses of dead mammals.

★ Rabies is spread by the saliva of an infected mammal, usually by a bite. However, fresh saliva in a cut or sore can also cause rabies — so don't touch your dog, cat, or other pet if you think it's been around a mammal that might have rabies, because your pet's fur might have fresh saliva on it from the infected animal.

★ If you've been bitten by a mammal, or think you've come in contact with any mammal that might have rabies, tell a grown-up AT ONCE. There is treatment, but you need to start it soon, so please don't wait.

These rules will make you a good, safe, smart wildlife observer and outdoorsperson.

NATIVE AMERICAN • LEGENDS •

Native Americans — the North American Indians — told many wonderful stories, or *legends*, about wildlife. Wildlife was all-important to American Indians, because they depended on it for food, clothing, and certain kinds of shelter. The Indians felt a great closeness to these wild creatures, whether it was prey such as rabbits, deer, and buffalo that they hunted for food and clothing, or whether it was their fellow predators, such as bobcats, coyotes, or wolves.

Indian legends served at least three purposes. First, they told of special characteristics that the Indians had observed about these creatures, such as the cleverness of the coyote. Second, they were a way of explaining things about wildlife, such as why the bear has such a short tail, or why the crane has long legs. Third, they were great entertainment — marvelous stories to be told and retold around the campfire. Fortunately, we can still enjoy these wonderful legends and learn these time-honored insights and observations, while imagining what it must have been like to hear them around an Indian campfire.

Ask Permission

Land such as national and state forests and parks is called *public* land. That's because the government holds it for all of us to enjoy. Except in a few special cases, you don't need permission to go on public lands.

But most land isn't public land; it's *private* land. That means it's owned by ordinary people like you and me. It's their property, just as much as your house and yard or your apartment are your property.

Most private landowners will let you look at wildlife on their land if you ask them politely and tell them you'll be careful not to cause any damage. That means you won't litter, leave gates open, cut down young trees, pick wildflowers, or do other things that might be destructive. Be sure to ask the landowner's permission first and then treat the land the way you'd like someone to treat your property!

Have Fun!

Now you're ready to have some very good times with wildlife — and that's what this book is all about! You can learn all kinds of fascinating things about wildlife from the ideas, activities, information, arts and crafts, and experiences in this book, and you'll have lots of fun doing it.

SMALL MAMMALS

Mammals come in all sizes, from the largest whale to the giant brown bear and moose to the shrew, which is so tiny that some kinds of shrew could almost fit in a thimble! All mammals have certain things in common, though, no matter what their size or shape.

For one thing, all mammals nurse their young on milk that their mothers produce. For another, they all have hair, although some mammals like whales and elephants have so little hair that we don't really notice it. Mammals are also warm-blooded. That means they burn enough food to keep their bodies warm at a steady temperature.

If you find yourself especially interested in mammals, it may be because you are a mammal, too. That's right — humans are mammals. Do you see how we fit into the mammal characteristics?

BATS

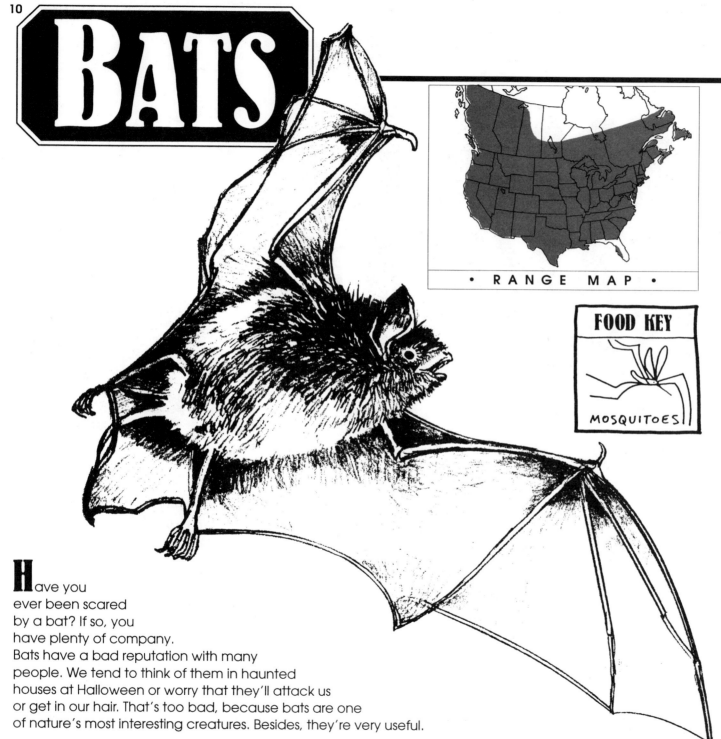

· RANGE MAP ·

FOOD KEY

MOSQUITOES

WHAT'S FOR DINNER?

If you were a bat, you could plan to munch about 600 mosquitoes in an hour! How's that for a hearty appetite — and a lot of work, too. One Texas bat cave houses 20 million to 30 million bats, and together, they eat 500 thousand pounds — that's 250 tons —·of insects each night. Imagine how many insects we'd have if there were no bats dining out every night!

How many mosquitoes?: Ask a grown-up if you can use a box of elbow macaroni. Pour the entire box into a large glass jar. These are your mosquitoes. Make a list of how many "mosquitoes" you, friends, and family guess are in your jar. Then ask someone to help you count them (put them in piles of 50 each). Who guessed the closest? Are there more or less than 600? As you can see, bats must be very busy to catch and eat as many mosquitoes and insects as they do. Keeping the insect population in check is a big help to the environment.

Have you ever been scared by a bat? If so, you have plenty of company. Bats have a bad reputation with many people. We tend to think of them in haunted houses at Halloween or worry that they'll attack us or get in our hair. That's too bad, because bats are one of nature's most interesting creatures. Besides, they're very useful.

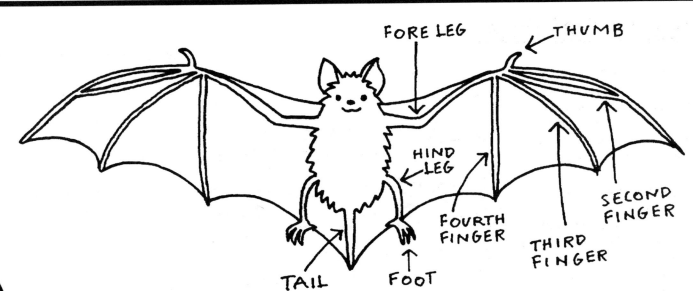

Do you know what a *mammal* is? Mammals are creatures that are warm-blooded, have hair on their bodies, and have young that nurse on their mother's milk. Humans are mammals, and so are bats. But bats aren't just any old mammal; bats are the ONLY mammal that truly flies!

Although bats may look like flying mice because they're small and furry, they really aren't like mice at all. In fact, they're actually more closely related to humans than to mice.

Some people are afraid of being attacked by a rabid bat. There's not much to worry about, though. Bats, unlike other animals with rabies, seldom attack other creatures. However, you should NEVER try to handle a bat — or any other wild mammal — especially one that acts sick. Leave bat handling to the experts!

Bats have been on earth for at least 60 million years. That means they developed only about 5 million years after the dinosaurs died out. It also means they've been around for about 57 million years longer than humans and our ancestors. Some scientists believe that bats evolved from small, shrewlike mammals that lived in trees and ate insects.

A closer look: If you make a set of bat wings out of heavy paper and straws or toothpicks, you will have a much clearer idea of how these mammals with wings use their curious appendages. Look at the drawing of bat wings; notice the thin bones in the wing. These bones are really the fingers of the bat's front paw or hand. You can put bones (not real ones, of course) on the underside of your bat wings. Use model airplane glue to fasten thin, flexible pieces of plastic (you can use straws or toothpicks) to the paper. Try to follow the same pattern of bones that you see in the picture. Can you imagine your fingers growing very long and thin and then being covered with a tough skin like a bat's wing?

Echolocation, or "Bat Radar"

Are you afraid a bat will dive right into you? Well, you'll be pleased to know that the last thing the bat wants to do is attack you or run into you. Bats almost never attack people or fly into their hair. In fact, bats avoid running into any object except the insects on which they feed.

They do this by using a remarkable system called *echolocation.* Flying bats constantly give off high-pitched squeaks that we can't even hear. They have very large ears; these help them hear the *echoes* coming back as the squeaks bounce off even the tiniest objects, so that they can instantly tell the *location* of the insects they eat. This is a lot like radar, only bats used it long before there were people on earth!

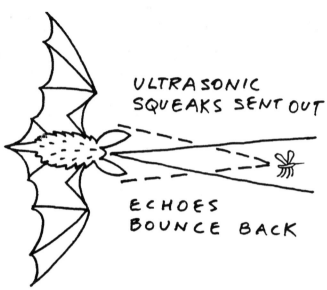

ULTRASONIC SQUEAKS SENT OUT

ECHOES BOUNCE BACK

The better to hear you with, my dear: Take a good look at the ears of a bat. What do you notice about the size and shape of the ears? Look at your ears in a mirror. How are they different from a bat's?

While one person sits in a chair and wears a blindfold, have another person ring a bell or clap hands from different locations. Can the blindfolded person point to the bell to identify its location?

Next have the blindfolded person cup his or her hands behind the ears and try again to locate the bell. What did the use of hands do? Look again at a picture of a bat's ears. How does the design of a bat's ears compare with the cupped hands at your ears?

RADAR GAME

Have you heard the expression "blind as a bat"? Well, don't you believe it! North American bats may not have outstanding eyesight, but they certainly aren't blind (many tropical bats have very good eyesight). Even though bats aren't blind, they do rely heavily on their radar and echolocation to find food and avoid objects in their paths.

Here's a game you can play with your friends in an open field or playground. While playing, you'll understand a little more about how bats get around. Begin by blindfolding one person in the group to be "It." This person must then try to tag the others in the group by listening to the bat squeaks the others make, and tagging them. The "squeakers" can't move and must squeak once the game begins. The last person to be tagged becomes "It."

ROOSTING BAT

Make a bat magnet to roost in your house to remind you of how useful these interesting creatures are.

Here's what you'll need:

Black, brown, or gray construction paper — 11½" x 3" strip and a triangular piece 6" x 4" x 4"

Clothespin — kind with metal spring

Glue, tape, newspaper

Tempera paint (black, brown, or gray, depending on bat species)

Small magnet

1. Spread newspaper on work space. Paint the clothespin and allow to dry. This is the bat's body.

2. Fold the strip of construction paper in half and draw a wing pattern on it, using wing illustration (see page 11) as a guide. Cut out the wings and glue onto the dry clothespin.

3. Pinch the triangle together as shown to form ears. Wrap in place with tape. Open the clothespin and tuck the ears back in against the metal spring. Put a drop of glue on one side to hold the ears in place.

4. Glue a magnet on the clothespin and place on refrigerator. Just squeeze the clothespin open and your bat can help you by holding important messages.

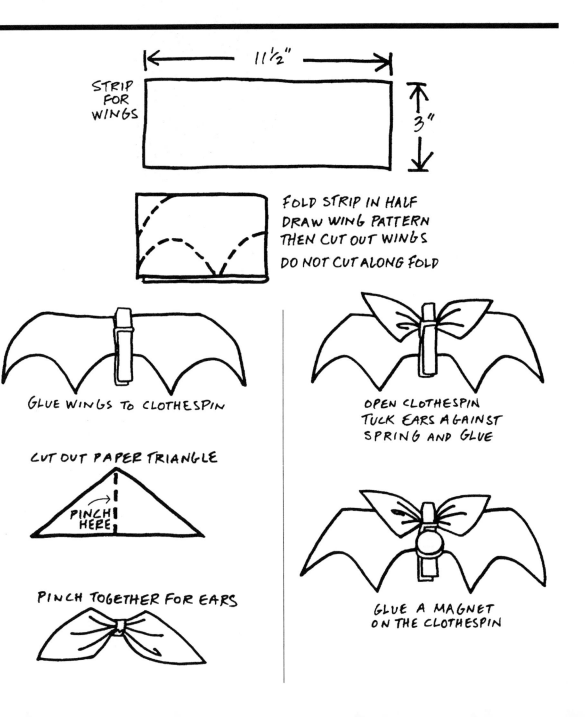

STRIP FOR WINGS — 11½" — 3"

FOLD STRIP IN HALF
DRAW WING PATTERN
THEN CUT OUT WINGS

DO NOT CUT ALONG FOLD

GLUE WINGS TO CLOTHESPIN

CUT OUT PAPER TRIANGLE
PINCH HERE

PINCH TOGETHER FOR EARS

OPEN CLOTHESPIN
TUCK EARS AGAINST
SPRING AND GLUE

GLUE A MAGNET
ON THE CLOTHESPIN

HOME SWEET HOME

All the bats in North America are *nocturnal*, which means they're active mostly at night. During the day, bats rest in different places. These places are called *bat roosts*.

Some *species* (kinds) of bats live in large colonies in caves or abandoned mine tunnels. Others hang singly among the leaves of trees, or in hollow trees or attics. All of them hang upside down, however, although no one is quite sure why. Apparently they evolved this way, with hind feet suited for clinging upside down, rather than developing like birds, with feet adapted for perching. Bats also use the clawlike thumb at the joint of the wing to cling to walls and balance them while roosting. Bats are the ONLY creature that roosts upside down!

A bat's point of view: Lie on your back on a bed and hang your head and shoulders down as far as you can toward the floor. Pretend that you're a roosting bat. Do things look strange and different when you're upside down? You may feel funny, because the blood rushes to your head, but bats are designed so that doesn't bother them. Hanging upside down seems normal to a bat!

FAMILY LIFE

Most kinds of bat have only one or two young each year. The babies of some species cling to their mother's fur with their feet and to one of her nipples — which are on the SIDE of her body — with their mouths during her night feeding flights. When they become too heavy (after a few days), she leaves them at the bat roost while she feeds. The young bats can usually fly when they are about four weeks old.

WHERE SHALL WE SPEND THE WINTER?

Some North American bats *hibernate*. This means they spend the winter in a very deep sleep inside a cave. Others fly to the southern United States or Central or South America to spend the winter where it's warmer. Do you know anyone who goes to Florida or some other warm place to spend the winter? Well, that's exactly what some bats do.

Bats You Might See

There are more than forty species of bats in North America. Some of these are so much alike that even experts have difficulty telling them apart, so don't worry if you can't tell one species of bat from another. One way to tell them apart is by their size. You'll probably be surprised at how small they are.

Small, smaller, smallest: You might think from its name that the *big brown bat* is rather large, but in fact a big one weighs just over half an ounce. How small is that? Cut a stick of butter or margarine into four pieces of equal size. Each of those pieces weighs one ounce. Now cut one of those pieces in half. Each of those little pieces weighs a half an ounce — and that's about as much as a big brown bat weighs!

Now, you may be wondering why it is called the big brown bat. Well, one reason is that the *little brown bat* (or *little brown myotis*) weighs only a quarter of an ounce. Cut the two half pieces of margarine in half again. One of those quarters is as big as the little brown bat. Cut those quarters in half yet again and you have the size of the *pipestrels* (both eastern and western).

Environmentally Yours

About 17 of the more than 40 species of bats in North America are considered by many scientists to be either endangered or threatened.

What can you do? Never disturb a bat roost or cave, especially in winter, when the bats are hibernating. Simply waking up a hibernating bat can use up to 67 days' worth of stored energy, so the bat may not survive the winter. Don't try to keep a bat as a pet; they almost always die quickly in captivity. Try to educate others that bats are good and should be protected. If you find a bat in your home, don't kill it. It's often a young bat that is confused. Leave windows open, and it will usually find its way out.

Learn more about bats: You can get lots of good information from your state Fish and Wildlife or Natural Resource Department, or from Bat Conservation International, P.O. Box 162603, Austin, TX 78716. The more you learn about bats, the more interesting you'll find them!

Night Watch

Early on a summer evening, at dusk, take a walk outside. If you live near a pond or lake, walk near there. A still, warm night is best; if the bugs are biting you, chances are the bats will be out feeding, too. Stand still and watch above you for flying bats. They like to dip and swoop, so don't be alarmed. How many bats did you see? What did you notice about how and where they swooped? Why do you think bats are helpful creatures?

Put up a bat house: Several major conservation organizations sell houses that are designed just for bats. (Write to Ted and Olympia LeBeau, 296 Brook Road, Springfield, VT 05156 or phone: 802-885-4007 to inquire about purchasing a bat house.) Now that you understand how useful bats are, you might want to attract some to your neighborhood. Don't be too disappointed if bats don't use your bat house for a roost, because bats can be very fussy about where they live. Still, if you put out two or three bat houses in locations with bat appeal, the chances are good that you'll attract some bats.

THE NINE-BANDED ARMADILLO

• RANGE MAP •

The armadillo is one of the strangest and most fascinating mammals found in North America. This odd little creature is only about the size of a house cat. It's covered with hard, horny plates. Whenever possible, the armadillo escapes danger by scuttling into brush so thick that most enemies can't follow it, or it dives into its burrow.

Its tough covering serves the armadillo very well, however, if it can't escape by running into a burrow or dense brush. Then it curls itself into a ball to protect its soft underside. In this position, it can also kick its enemies very hard with its strong hind legs and long claws. This defense makes many enemies think twice about having armadillo for dinner!

The armadillo belongs to a special group of mammals that includes sloths and anteaters. Most armadillos live in South and Central America, but the nine-banded armadillo also lives in a small section of the southwestern United States.

Fun reads: Ask at the library for *Just So Stories: The Beginning of the Armadillo* by Rudyard Kipling.

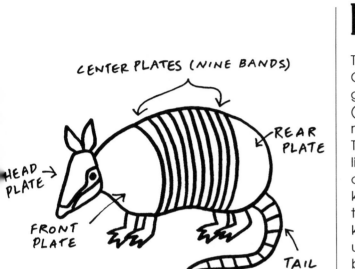

CENTER PLATES (NINE BANDS)

HEAD PLATE →

REAR PLATE

FRONT PLATE

TAIL PLATES

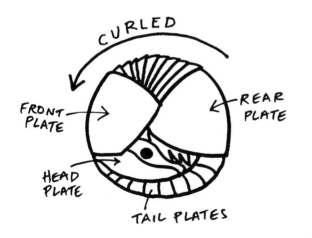

CURLED

FRONT PLATE →

REAR PLATE

HEAD PLATE

TAIL PLATES

Look at My Armor

The first Europeans to come to South and Central America were Spanish, and they gave the armadillo its name. Armadillo (pronounced arma-DEE-yo in Spanish) means *little armed* (or armored) *one.* The armadillo does indeed look almost like an animal in a suit of armor, and the comparison isn't silly. The armor worn by knights in olden days had big plates held together by flexible joints, so that the knights could move. Well, the armadillo uses much the same system. It has one big plate covering the front part of its body, another big plate covering the rear, and nine flexible bands in the middle of its body. These bands, of course, give our armadillo its name of "nine-banded."

Let's compare: Look at pictures in a library book or an encyclopedia of the armor that knights used to wear, or go to a museum that has real suits of armor on display. Then study the armor worn by turtles and armadillos. Which animal has armor that is the most like the armor humans used? Think of the advantages and disadvantages that each kind of armor has. Which kind of armor would you rather have, and why?

HOME SWEET HOME

Create An Armadillo Sculpture

Sometimes the best way to really understand how something works is by trying to create one of your own. It doesn't have to look exactly like an armadillo to be helpful to you.

Look at the illustrations in this book, and if you want, look for some more armadillo pictures. Then gather some materials and go to it. (You might want to use some old aluminum foil for the basic body shape, and then make armored plates to glue on from paper plates or old paper egg cartons.) That should get you started. Be as detailed and creative as you like.

The armadillo digs long burrows, 10 to 15 feet in length. It can dig very fast with its powerful front legs and long, strong front claws. In fact, an armadillo can dig its way right out of sight in just a minute or two if the ground isn't too hard! Armadillos also find dens in rocky outcroppings. They often live in very dry country, and they like to hang around streams and water holes, where they can drink and take mud baths.

Desert life: Have you ever wondered how animals living in the desert get the water they need to survive, if a stream or water hole isn't nearby? Well, believe it or not, very dry or sandy soil contains enough water for living things to survive in many places. This experiment will show you why this is true.

Here's what you'll need:

Large bucket of sand, or ground with dry or sandy soil
Large piece of plastic wrap (reuse old piece)
Paper cup
Small stones

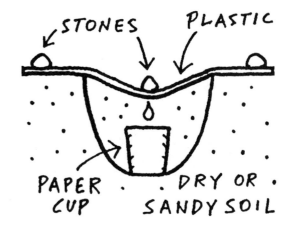

In a sunny area, dig a 2-foot-deep hole in the sand or bucket. Place the cup in the bottom of the hole. Cover the top with plastic wrap, leaving a dip in the center of it. Weight the edges down with a few stones. Place a small stone in the center of the plastic wrap over the cup.

Let set for a few hours. Notice how water forms on the wrap and drips into the cup. This is called *condensation*. Here's how it happens: The sun heats the water in the sand; the water then *evaporates* into the air. When it hits the plastic wrap, it is trapped, and as it cools down it *condenses*, or forms a liquid, water. So even where it seems there is no water, there is actually moisture available to animals, like the armadillo, that can burrow deep into the ground.

Automobiles are the armadillo's worst enemy. Its armor doesn't do it any good when it's run over by a car or a truck. However, there are plenty of armadillos, so there's no danger right now that this interesting little animal will become extinct.

WHAT'S FOR DINNER?

Armadillos are *omnivorous*, which means they'll eat all kinds of things, but most of these don't require sharp, strong teeth for heavy chewing. They have very primitive teeth that are almost like pegs. They have a long, sticky tongue, however, much like an anteater's; this is very handy for slurping up termites and other insects. Besides insects, armadillos eat a few fruits and berries, birds' eggs, and sometimes feed on the carcasses of dead animals.

Valuable tongues: The armadillo has a *prehensile* tongue, which means it is designed, or *adapted*, to seize and grasp things, and wrap itself around things like food. Compare what your tongue is designed to do with that of the armadillo. Can you roll it? Can you fold it? Can you actually pick things up with it? What happens to your tongue when you talk? Try to talk without moving your tongue. Though used very differently, you and the armadillo have special tongue designs, or adaptations, that work best to meet the needs of each of you.

FAMILY LIFE

There are many strange and interesting things about the armadillo, but none more curious than the fact that it has four young that are either all male or all female. Wouldn't it be a strange and different world if all human mothers had either four boys or four girls?

All of a kind: Make a list of some of your friends and their brothers and sisters. Then think what their families might be like if each girl had three sisters and no brothers, or if each boy had three brothers and no sisters. Which families would stay the same? What about you and your family? Does this make you glad you're not an armadillo?

Meet My Relative, the Glyptodont

The earliest fossils of armadillos date back about 55 million years ago. That's only about 10 million years after the dinosaurs became extinct, so armadillos have been around for a very, very long time. It's no wonder they're almost like prehistoric fossils!

Glyptodonts (GLIP-toe-donts), now extinct, were close relatives of the armadillo. Instead of flexible shells like the armadillo's, they had a shell much like a turtle's. One kind of glyptodont had an amazing tail. It was fairly long and slender, like an armadillo's, but it had a huge ball at the end, covered with sharp spikes. Probably the glyptodont lashed its enemies with this club, much as armored knights used a terrible weapon with a spiked ball, called a mace. It seems that our knights in shining armor took a lot of ideas from the armadillo and its relatives.

THE OPOSSUM

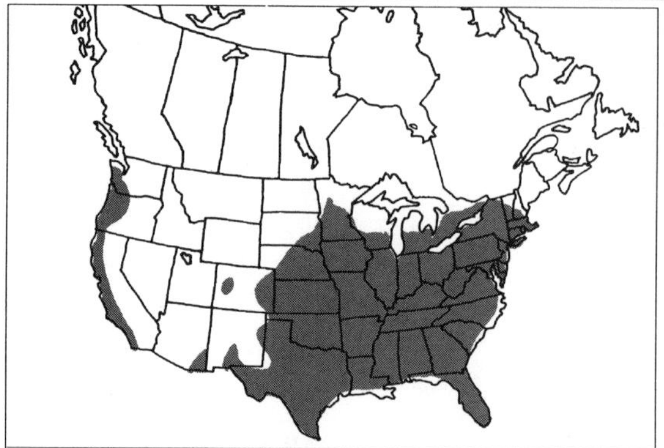

In Virginia, in 1612, the famous Captain John Smith became the first European to describe an opossum, or *possum*, as it is known for short. He wrote, in what seems to us the strange spelling of that time, "An Opassum hath a head like a Swine, & a taile like a rat, and is of the Bignes of a Cat."

That's a very good description. It's not hard to tell a possum when you see one for the first time. With its long, naked tail, it looks a little like a rat, although it's a lot bigger — about the size of a house cat, in fact. The base of its tail is black, and so are its short, rounded ears. It has a very long, pointed face that's nearly white, with a pink nose at the end. The fur on its body is usually light gray in the North, but is often darker in the South.

• R A N G E   M A P •

FOOD KEY

PERSIMMONS

MICE

WORMS

GARBAGE

BIRDS' EGGS

NUTS

A mouthful: The possum has 50 teeth — that's more than any other mammal that isn't a marsupial. How many do other mammals have? Try to count your teeth? Ask your friends how many teeth they think a dog, a cat, a mouse, or a whale has? Then ask a grown-up to help you look in the encyclopedia to find out the number of teeth these mammals actually have. How close were you and your friends?

FAMILY LIFE

A North American Marsupial

The opossum is a *marsupial*, which is a mammal that carries its tiny young in a pouch until they're big enough to come out into the world. Marsupials are among the world's most primitive mammals, but they seem to have been highly successful in surviving for a very long time. One advantage marsupials have is that they can carry their babies with them. This allows the mother to search for food in a much larger area than she could if she had to return often to a den to feed her young.

Marsupials are common in Central and South America, and of course, Australia is famous for such marsupials as the kangaroo and koala. However, the opossum is the only marsupial found in North America.

Like all marsupials, possum babies are so tiny and undeveloped that they couldn't possibly survive without the protection of their mother's pouch. They're born blind, deaf, and hairless.

Right after birth, the tiny possums travel about *two inches* to the pouch, where they nurse on their mother's milk for about three months. Some of the babies can't even manage to travel that two inches, and die before they reach the pouch.

Wherever their mother goes (and she travels a long way each night looking for food), her babies ride with her in the pouch. Male possums go their separate way after mating and have nothing to do with raising the young possums.

After about three months, the young possums come out of the pouch. About a week later, they begin traveling with their mother on her nightly feeding expeditions. Often they'll ride by clinging to her long fur (not by hanging from her tail), but sometimes they'll scamper along beside her. Then, after a few more weeks, they're on their own.

So very tiny: Newborn possums are no bigger than a raisin. They're so tiny that a teaspoon can hold an entire litter of them!

Try it: Fill a teaspoon with 10 – 15 raisins. Can you believe how tiny these creatures are? No wonder they are such fragile newborns.

Make a Pouch

If your parents are like most busy people, they probably carried you around in a basket or baby backpack when you were first born. It allowed them to keep an eye on you, while tending to their daily tasks.

Make your own cloth pouch to hold items that are special to you. With some felt, a needle, and thread, you can make a soft little pouch to wear as a necklace or attach to your belt.

Here's what you'll need:

Felt, 2 pieces 5" x 5"
Large needle and thread, or glue
Hole punch and yarn

Place the two felt pieces together. If you sew, thread the needle and begin sewing down one end, around, and up the other side with a simple loop stitch. Leave the top side open. Use the illustration as a guide. Knot the end. (Or, glue three sides together. Place under a heavy book until the glue dries.) Punch two holes in the felt as shown, and pass the yarn through each one. Tie the ends, and wear your handy pouch. Glue on some glitter, ribbon, or colorful felt designs, if you wish.

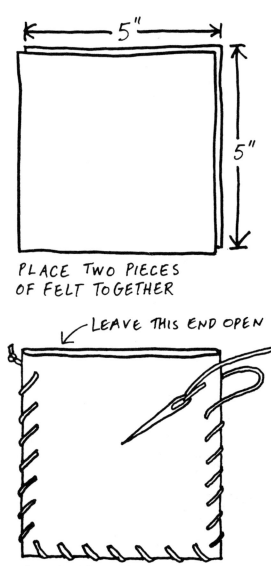

PLACE TWO PIECES OF FELT TOGETHER

LEAVE THIS END OPEN

LOOP STITCH AROUND THREE SIDES

DECORATE YOUR POUCH

NATIVE AMERICAN LEGENDS

Opossum is the name which Native Americans gave this animal, and it's not surprising that they had legends about something that was so common in parts of North America. The Creek Indians, who lived in what are now Alabama and neighboring states, created an interesting legend to explain how the possum got his long, naked, ratlike tail.

The possum wanted to be as handsome as the raccoon, so he painted a mask on his face. But the other animals just made fun of him, so he decided that he wanted his furry tail to have rings, like the raccoon's.

Possum asked the raccoon how to have a ringed tail, and the raccoon told him to wrap strips of bark around his tail and then hold his tail in the fire. Possum did this, but the fire burned all the hair off his tail, and his tail remains naked to this very day!

Tell a tale: Imagine that you're an American Indian of long ago, entertaining your people with stories around the fire at night. Make up your own legend about why the possum has such a long, pointed face with so many teeth. Use your imagination to create the most interesting story you can think of.

LIFE CAN BE SHORT

One of the most unusual things about this unusual animal is its short life span. For its adult size, the opossum is one of the shortest-lived animals in the world. A house cat often lives for 15 years or more, but possums in the wild rarely live to be more than 2 years old — and most don't even last that long. Why? No one knows for sure, but possums seem to live life at a very fast pace and wear out quickly.

Even so, the species has been able to survive because the females have so many babies at an early age. The mother has her first litter of 10 – 15 babies when she's only 6 – 9 months old. If she lives long enough, she'll have another litter in another 6 – 9 months.

PLAYING POSSUM

Have you ever heard the expression "playing possum"? It means keeping so still that something seems to be dead. Some people think that the opossum plays dead when it's in danger. Possums often do appear to be dead when they really aren't, but they're not exactly pretending. The possum, with its very small brain, isn't smart enough to think, or pretend. Instead, it just reacts automatically, much like you do when you blink when someone waves a hand in front of your face. This is called a *reflex action*.

A possum threatened by a predator first shows its mouthful of sharp teeth, growls, and hisses almost like an angry cat. If that doesn't work, the possum may try to run away. But if the predator, such as a dog, coyote, or human, grabs the possum, it goes limp with its eyes wide open and seems to be dead. Sometimes this works, and the predator loses interest; the possum may continue to appear dead for several hours.

Coyote and possum game: Here's something you can play with two or more people — the more people (opossums), the funnier it gets. Put on some favorite music; all the opossums then dance away with all sorts of silly gyrations. The person who is the Coyote suddenly turns the music off, and the possums must freeze into total stillness. Don't move a muscle; don't change to a more comfortable position. Coyote walks around and tries to make you smile, laugh, move, scratch an itch. If you do, Coyote will have caught you and you will be out. Last one left gets to be Coyote next time.

Using Its Feet

The possum is said to sleep while hanging by its tail, but biologists who spend a great deal of time watching wild possums have never seen this done. Possums sometimes wrap their long tails around a branch, but they do this more for balance than to hang by the tail. The confusion is probably because of the possum's unusual hind feet. Four of its toes have sharp claws, but the fifth has no nail and is placed almost like the thumb on a human or a monkey. This means that the possum can grip a branch with its hind feet just the way a monkey can with its front feet. A possum can easily hang from a branch by its hind feet, and it's these feet, rather than its tail, which make the possum such a great climber.

• RANGE MAP •

RANGE MAPS

As you've noticed, there are range maps for each animal in this book. These maps tell you where each animal species lives in North America. It is important to first find where you live on the map. That way you will know if there is likely to be a chance for you to see a particular type of wildlife near where you live. Perhaps you visit a grandparent or good friend in another part of the country. Begin noticing which animal species you might look for on your next visit.

Occasionally you'll hear about an unusual sighting of an animal — perhaps because of a mild winter. Well, the opossum has actually permanently changed its range over the years. It was once mostly seen in the southeastern United States, although it came as far north as Ohio, Indiana, and Virginia. Since then, however, the possum has steadily increased its range. This may be due partly to a very gradual warming of the climate. Also, people have carried possums to new places without realizing it by car and plane. So keep an eye out; you never know when you will see an animal out of its traditional range.

Where are we?: After you find yourself on the range map, flip through this book and draw a picture of each animal that lives where you do. Post this on your refrigerator so that you will know what animals to look for when you go out exploring.

HOME SWEET HOME

Possums usually rest in some sort of den. Like their taste in food, possums aren't fussy about a den, as long as it provides some shelter and protection from enemies. A possum den can be in a hollow tree or log, an underground burrow, an old woodchuck hole, a brush pile, a culvert, or even underneath a building. Possums often use a number of dens, too. As they roam around their territory in search of food, they may sleep in one den for a night or two, then move on to another, and then to still another. It doesn't matter to the possum, as long as it can find food nearby.

FUN FACTS

Marsupial ancestors of the possum were among the early mammals. The oldest marsupial fossil was found in Alberta, Canada and is about 85 million years old. That means that marsupials evolved during the age of dinosaurs. At that time, most of the continents were part of one huge land mass which we now call *Gondwanaland.*

THE RACCOON

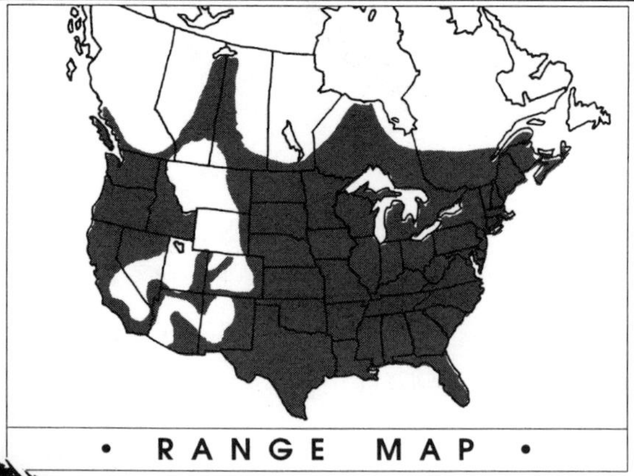

RANGE MAP

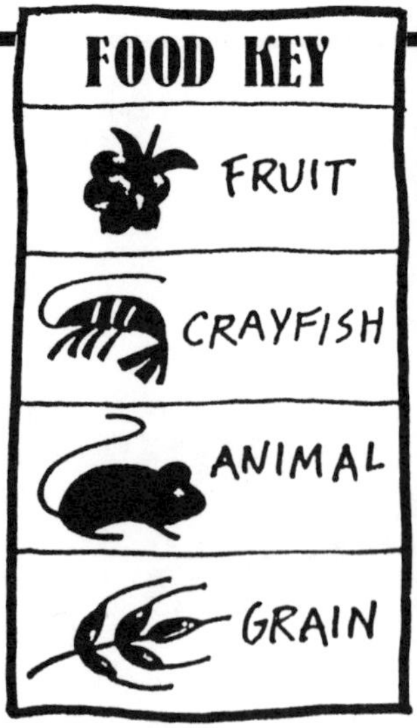

FOOD KEY

- FRUIT
- CRAYFISH
- ANIMAL
- GRAIN

Pretty Hand-y!

Raccoons have little front paws — almost like hands — so they can open many things that other animals can't. Whether it's opening a mussel at the edge of a stream, pulling ears of corn off the stalks, prying the lids off garbage cans — no matter how tightly and cleverly they are closed — or reaching into a nest for birds' eggs, a raccoon depends a great deal on the use of its front paws.

PAW PRINT SOCKS

If you've walked along the muddy edge of a pond, lake, or stream, or in the wet snow, you've probably discovered *imprints,* or tracks, made by animals living in or around those areas. Looking for paw prints is a wonderful way to learn what species of wildlife live in your neck of the woods — or in your busy city!

Look closely at the raccoon imprints at the top of this page. Do you see anything familiar? You're right — raccoons have the same number of toes as people! These socks, with true-to-life raccoon prints painted on the bottoms, will help you remember how raccoon tracks look next time you're out exploring.

Here's what you'll need:

Pair of white, cotton socks

Newspapers and scrap paper

Strip of cardboard to slip sock over

No.1 (extra soft lead) pencil

Fabric paint, any color, and paintbrush

1. Cover your work area with newspapers. Practice sketching raccoon paw prints on scrap paper. Use the prints on this page as a model. Make a paw template to trace, if you want.

2. Now, stretch a sock over a piece of cardboard so the surface of the sock is flat. Outline the paw print on the sock bottom with the pencil. Fill in the paw outline with fabric paint — wild colors are fun — and let dry completely. Remove the cardboard. Repeat for the other sock paw print. If you make these on heavy socks, they become a great pair of slippers!

REAR PAW PRINT

FRONT PAW PRINT

Food For Thought

Have you ever dipped your cookies in milk? Do you eat your cereal with milk poured over it? Raccoons, like people, have certain ways they eat foods, too. In fact, raccoons have a peculiar habit of dunking some of their food in water before eating it, but they aren't really trying to wash it, as a lot of people believe. Most likely, this is an *instinctive* act (something they do without learning), developed because dipping food in water makes it easier to chew and swallow. Raccoons eat lots of food that isn't near water, too. In fact, raccoons enjoy the food at the restaurant found near many homes. You guessed it — the garbage can!

What do you think?: Next time you're shopping with Mom or Dad, ask them to buy some dried apples and crunchy cookies, like ginger snaps, for a home experiment. At snack time, or after dinner, taste each food. Is it dry or tough to eat? Now, dip an apple slice in apple juice and the cookie in milk. Are they easier to chew and swallow? Can you see why raccoons enjoy dipping their food in water?

"Cute" Doesn't Mean Safe

People often think that wild animals, especially baby raccoons, look cute and cuddly, with their fat, furry, ringed tail and the dark patches around their eyes that look like a mask. But "cute" and "cuddly" are human terms, and wild animals don't live by human rules. Just because we think an animal looks cute, it doesn't mean that it's safe to pet, handle, or raise as a pet.

There's another very important reason never to handle raccoons. They are very likely to carry rabies during an epidemic. In fact, one particular *strain* (kind) of the rabies virus is actually called the *raccoon strain* by scientists. Never, NEVER go near a raccoon, especially one that acts sick or mean. If you see a raccoon behaving strangely, ask a grown-up to call your local conservation officer or animal control office immediately. So, enjoy watching raccoons from a safe distance, but don't touch them or pick them up.

FUN FACTS

Fossils of animals related to the raccoon date back to about fifteen million (15,000,000) years ago. That's not nearly as old as dinosaurs, or even bats (60,000,000 years ago), but it's older than some mammals.

HOME SWEET HOME

In the wild, away from humans, raccoons usually have a den in a hollow tree, although they sometimes live in hollow logs, holes in piles of rocks, or even a burrow in the ground. Near humans, they can find all kinds of places for dens — attics, old barns, underneath outbuildings, unused chimneys, culverts, hollow partitions in walls, and overhead spaces in garages. They aren't fussy, as long as they can find a place to hide and have some shelter if the weather is very cold.

WHERE SHALL WE SPEND THE WINTER?

Like bears, raccoons put on a lot of fat in the fall, but they don't really *hibernate*. They do, however, stay in a den for much of the winter, especially where the climate is cold, using up a lot of the extra fat that they've stored. They're awake most of the time, though, and if there's a really warm spell, the raccoons will come out and hunt for food. The young may go off and find their own dens in the fall, or they may den with the mother as a group during the winter.

How BIG is BIG

Raccoons are medium-sized mammals. Adults are two and a half to more than three feet long, including the tail. They weigh around 15 – 25 pounds — about twice the weight of most house cats.

Weigh in: If you can, try weighing your cat on a scale. First weigh yourself. Then weigh yourself with a cat in your arms. Subtract your weight alone from the combined weight to get your cat's weight. Draw a 6" line with a ruler, with every inch equaling 10 pounds. Mark your cat's weight, the raccoon's weight (about 25 pounds), and your weight. That should give you a clearer idea of how heavy a raccoon is. It helps to be able to visualize (see) things in order to really understand them.

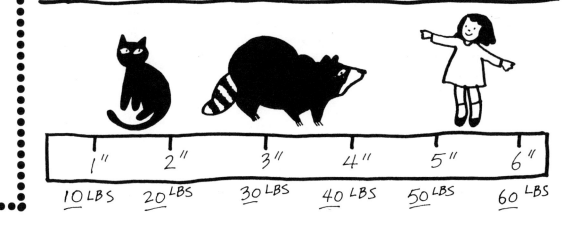

1"	2"	3"	4"	5"	6"
10 LBS	20 LBS	30 LBS	40 LBS	50 LBS	60 LBS

Environmentally Yours

Raccoons are extremely good at finding the nests of birds, whether they're on the ground, nestled in the branches of trees, or in hollows in tree trunks. Because there are now so many raccoons, they can do a lot of damage to the *populations* (numbers) of many kinds of birds, especially songbirds like robins, bluebirds, and thrushes, and waterfowl including ducks and geese.

While it's normal for a *predator* such as the raccoon to *prey on*, or hunt, these birds and their eggs, it's NOT normal to have so many raccoons. It's only because of us humans and our activities — providing places for raccoons to live and plenty of garbage for them to eat — that there are so many raccoons, now. Can you believe that one farmer actually had 26 raccoons living in his barn, and 34 raccoons were found in an attic over an apartment! Think how many birds' eggs they can eat! How do you think we can best protect song-birds, ducks, and geese from the over-population of raccoons?

"MASK"- QUERADE

The word *camouflage,* derived from the French word *camoufler,* meaning "to disguise," is important in our understanding of how animals protect themselves from predators. Raccoons, with their black-masked faces and ringed tails against their brown-black fur, have a natural camouflage that helps hide them from predators. See how their colors seem to melt right into the shadows of trees and wooded areas.

Here's a fun way to turn a grocery bag into a raccoon mask you can wear!

Here's what you'll need:

Brown paper grocery bag

Scissors and hole punch

Pencil, black marker, white crayon, and glue

String or thin ribbon

1. Cut the grocery bag open along the side corners and top so it lies flat. Cut away the back of the bag and save for whiskers.

2. Using the illustration as a guide, draw the outline of a raccoon's face (along with the mask's side bands) on the bag. Color in the raccoon's mask with the marker. Cut out the whole mask. Cut two holes for eyes.

3. Cut 10 thin paper strips, about 3" long, from the extra piece of paper bag. Glue 5 strips at each edge of the face for whiskers.

4. When glue is dry, punch two holes at the end of each side band. Loop string through holes and tie so mask is held securely around your head. If you write a folk tale about raccoons, you can act it out using the mask you made.

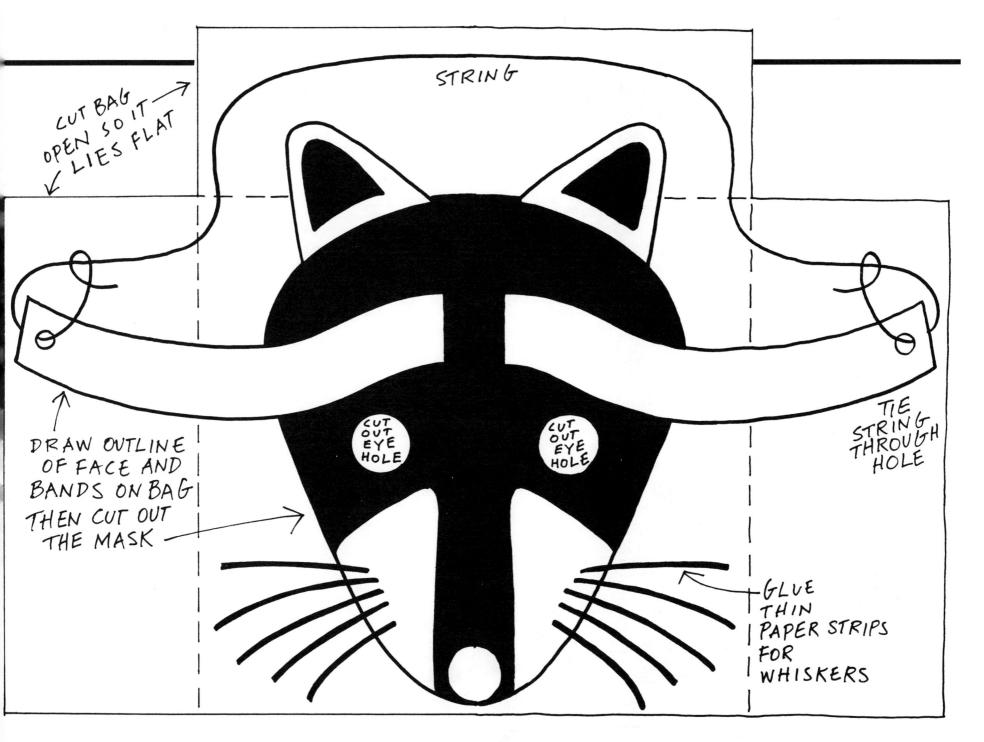

STRING

CUT BAG OPEN SO IT LIES FLAT

DRAW OUTLINE OF FACE AND BANDS ON BAG THEN CUT OUT THE MASK

CUT OUT EYE HOLE

CUT OUT EYE HOLE

TIE STRING THROUGH HOLE

GLUE THIN PAPER STRIPS FOR WHISKERS

Keeping Our Balance

What happens when a friend who is just about your size gets on the seesaw with you at your favorite park or playground? Sometimes you are in perfect balance; other times, as when two people are on one end and you are on the other, you go flying high — almost falling off — and they sink right to the ground because you are not well-balanced anymore. Well, that is something like the *balance of nature,* and what is happening to the song-birds and raccoons. No, they don't ride seesaws, but the size of their populations used to be in fairly good balance so that there were enough songbirds for the raccoons to eat, but not so many raccoons that they would eat too many songbirds. Nature usually can take care of itself and keep things in balance, but when we humans get involved — by providing garbage that raccoons eat — it's like putting an extra person on the seesaw and the balance is thrown off.

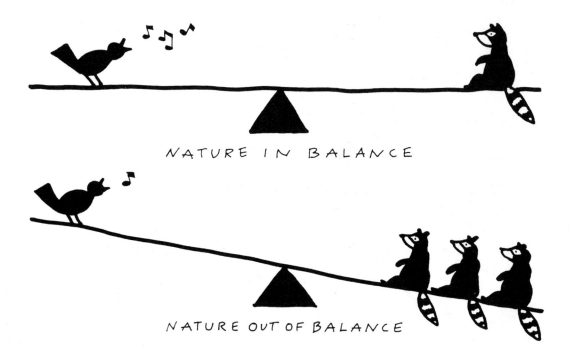

NATURE IN BALANCE

NATURE OUT OF BALANCE

A WALK ON THE WILD SIDE

Imagine that you're a raccoon, and go for a walk to see how many kinds of food you can find. Mussels, crayfish, frogs, birds' eggs are favorite foods of raccoons. However, raccoons are true *omnivores* which means they eat meat and veg-etables. Actually, they will eat almost anything they can find — berries, fruit, nuts, grain, and your leftover pizza! Try to take your walk through different types of *habitat* — fields, brush, forest land, and especially the shallow edges of a pond, marsh, or quiet stream. Remember that if you were really a raccoon you'd eat just about anything that could possibly be eaten. If you live in a city, walk around your neighborhood, and try to see what a raccoon might enjoy for dinner. Look for raccoon tracks around water in soft, smooth mud during your walk.

Draw pictures of different kinds of food that raccoons might eat. How many kinds of raccoon food can you think of?

•

FAMILY LIFE

Raccoons have fairly large litters — usually four or five babies, but sometimes as many as seven at a time. These are born in April or May and stay in the den for about two months. Then they begin to travel with their mother each night as she goes out to forage for food. (Raccoons are *nocturnal* which means they prefer nighttime and rarely come out in the daytime.) The male 'coon has nothing to do with raising the young.

Follow the Biologist

Some raccoons have learned to follow the tracks of biologists who are checking bird nesting boxes. The raccoon then robs the eggs from the nest when the ranger leaves. How good would you be at spotting a sneaking raccoon? Here's a game to play with a group of at least three people. You'll need an old tennis ball or a piece of cloth to be the "egg."

Choose one person to be the Biologist. Everyone else is a Raccoon and stands behind a starting line about 10' - 15' away. The object is for a Raccoon to steal the "egg" from the Biologist without being caught. The Biologist places the "egg" near his feet, with his back to the "egg" and all the Raccoons. As the Biologist counts aloud to 3, the Raccoons creep forward. On "3" the Raccoons must crouch and freeze, while the Biologist quickly turns. If the Biologist catches a Raccoon moving, that Raccoon returns to the starting line. The Raccoon who is able to snatch the "egg" without getting caught is the next Biologist.

Tell a Tale

The raccoon's name comes from a Native American word, arakunem (ah-rah-KOO-nem). European settlers gradually came to pronounce it as "raccoon," and now many people simply shorten it to 'coon.

Imagine that you are a young Native American, growing up very much in tune with nature. You might frequently spot or hear a raccoon. Use your imagination to make up a story or legend about how the raccoon got its black mask. The language in legends is usually very simple and direct, often with a lesson, or moral, to the story. Is your story going to be funny, silly, or serious?

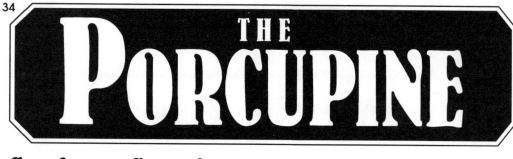

THE PORCUPINE

Curious Creatures

Have you ever seen a porcupine? Lots of people have, because porkies, as they are often called, are fairly common in much of North America. Besides, they're quite easy to see because they're large, slow-moving rodents that spend a lot of time in trees. Although they look awkward when they climb, porkies have always been considered good tree climbers. Biologists have now discovered, however, that porkies fall out of trees quite often and are sometimes seriously injured or even killed by the fall. Porcupines climb up a tree head first, but they back down a tree tail first.

Porkies, one of our largest rodents, grow to be as much as two and a half feet long and can weigh thirty pounds. They are dark colored — all but their quills, that is, which are mostly white, except for the pointed black tip. Porkies have quills only on the back, sides, and tail, but not on the face or underside. In addition to quills, they also have fur, particularly the long hairs on their back. They have very poor eyesight and probably can't see anything clearly beyond a few feet. They do have an excellent sense of smell, however, and can also hear quite well.

William Shakespeare wrote plays four hundred years ago that are still performed today. In one of his plays, he wrote about "quills upon the fretful *porpentine*." Isn't that an interesting old-fashioned spelling?

• RANGE MAP •

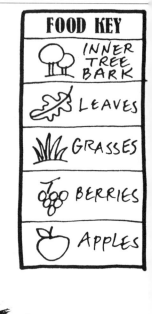

FOOD KEY

INNER TREE BARK

LEAVES

GRASSES

BERRIES

APPLES

SHARP AS A TACK

The porcupine gets its name from the Italian *porco* (pig) and *spino* (spine or quill). Even today you'll hear some people call a porcupine a *quill pig*. And it's no wonder that people are always curious about their quills — there are more than 30,000 quills on an adult porcupine! That's a lot of ammunition, and those quills are powerful weapons that protect the porky from many predators.

A porcupine absolutely cannot shoot its quills like arrows, as many mistakenly believe, but it may seem that way to its victims. A porky slaps with its tail and drives in a whole lot of quills so fast that it's no wonder some people think the animal is throwing its quills!

Have you ever watched a balloon go down when the air is let out of it? Some people think that a porcupine quill will shrink like that if the end is cut off, and then the quill will be easy to pull out. That's a bad mistake. Porcupine quills are filled with a spongy material, not air, and they don't shrink or soften if the end is cut off. Cutting off the end just makes the quill even harder to get hold of and remove. If a pet of yours tangles with a porcupine, you will probably need to take it to a veterinarian to have the quills safely removed.

Spy on a Porcupine

Porcupines love salt, and that often gets them in trouble with humans. Have you ever noticed how salty your sweat tastes? That's because there is salt in sweat, and the salt remains after the sweat dries up. To get salt, porkies will chew up almost anything humans have touched with sweaty hands, such as axe handles, canoe paddles, boots, gloves, the edges of doors, and countless other things which can cause them to be very destructive to people's homes, too.

If you live where there are porcupines, go into the woods and see if you can find one, or signs of one. Look for places where the bark has been chewed off trees, especially around rocky places where there might be porky dens. Late fall to early spring is the best time to look for porkies, because they're easier to see when the leaves are off the trees.

Added Impact

Have you ever noticed the barb on a fish hook? That's the sharp little piece that sticks out behind the point of the hook to keep it from coming out of the fish. Well, porcupines have tiny scales like fish scales — lots of them — on each quill, and these scales act just like the barbs on a fish hook. Although the scales are so tiny that you can't see them without a very strong magnifying glass, they hold the quills tightly in the predator that gets stuck with them, and come loose from the porcupine. Because of the muscle action and the scales, the quills work into the victim. It's very painful, and sometimes a predator will die if quills reach a vital spot.

A quill experiment: Ask a grown-up to help to make tiny cuts near the tip of a round toothpick. A very sharp knife or razor blade works best (please don't try this yourself). The knife should be pushed toward the tip, so that the end of the toothpick has tiny scales or barbs. Now you take over: Take a plain toothpick and push it through a piece of cloth or into a pin cushion. Then push in the toothpick with the scales. Try to pull each one out. Which one is harder to pull out? How does this make the porky's quills a better defensive weapon?

HAVE AN ADULT MAKE TINY CUTS

ROUND TOOTHPICK

TIP

CLOTH

PLAIN TOOTHPICK

CUT TOOTHPICK

CLOTH

QUILL TIP

SCALES

Porky says, "I dare you!"

Almost all large predators — bears, wolves, bobcats, coyotes, mountain lions, badgers, and wolverines — will occasionally kill a porcupine, but they don't do it very frequently. All too often they get a dose of quills, and that teaches them a painful lesson. Only the fisher kills porcupines regularly, and it's very good at it. (For more on the fisher and porcupine, see page 63.) Porcupines used to be a destructive nuisance in areas where the fisher was scarce, but now fishers have been brought back to most places where there are porcupines, keeping the population under natural control.

What's the Difference?

There are a lot of wildlife species that get confused with other species. Porcupines, for example, are often called hedgehogs, but the two aren't even related. The hedgehog is an insect-eating European mammal, much smaller than a porcupine. It's covered with sharp spines that help protect it from predators, but these spines aren't like a porcupine's quills, because they don't pull out of the hedgehog and work into the flesh of the attacker. Probably the porcupine was called a hedgehog because European settlers thought it was something like the hedgehogs they were familiar with.

Match up: Make a set of match-up cards from 3" x 5" index cards. For each species you include, make one card with a picture of the animal, and a separate card where you draw or write some of its characteristics that make it different from other animals. Think of animals that often get confused such as the porcupine and the hedgehog, the rat and the opossum, the toad and the frog, the crow and the raven. Add others from this book like the fox, wolf, deer, moose. Once you have all the cards made, mix them up, turn them all face down, and see if you can match the right cards to the right characteristics. The player with the most matched sets is the winner!

HOME SWEET HOME

Porcupines spend a lot of time in a den, which is usually a small cave or deep crevice in a ledge or rock pile, a large hollow in a tree trunk, a hollow under a partly uprooted tree, or an abandoned animal burrow. In very cold weather or deep snow, porkies sometimes stay in their den for two or three days at a time, but they're active for most of the winter. A porcupine lives alone for most of the year, but several may den together in the winter. When porkies are out of their dens, it's usually for a feeding expedition.

HEDGEHOG

PORCUPINE

NATIVE AMERICAN LEGENDS

Many Native American tribes thought very highly of the porcupine, so it's no surprise that the porky was sometimes a hero in their stories. The Tsimshian tribe of the Pacific Northwest thought the porcupine was very wise, as this tale shows.

The Tsimshian were great hunters who hunted for food throughout the year. Some of the animals thought this was unfair, so the grizzly bear called a meeting of all the animals. He suggested that the animals ask the Great Spirit for more cold in winter. "Then," he said, "the Tsimshian hunters would have to stay in their houses and not disturb the animals in their dens."

But the porcupine was wise and said that too much cold would kill the plants, and then the animals would starve. Then the animals agreed that it should be cold for six months and warm for six months, much as it is now. They made the porcupine their Wise Man, and they went into their dens during cold weather. However, the porcupine doesn't hide in its den for the winter, but goes about visiting his neighbors during cold weather.

Native American art: Native Americans used porcupine quills for decorations on their birch bark canoes, baskets, and buckskin clothing. They made beautiful designs with them and sometimes painted them to add color. Toothpicks (the round kind, not the flat ones) are about the same size and shape as a porcupine quill. Get a box of these, paint your toothpicks in bright colors, and make up designs of your own. It may help if you look in a book on American Indian craft (see *The Kids' Multicultural Art Book* by Alexandra Terzian) to see what sorts of designs the Indians made.

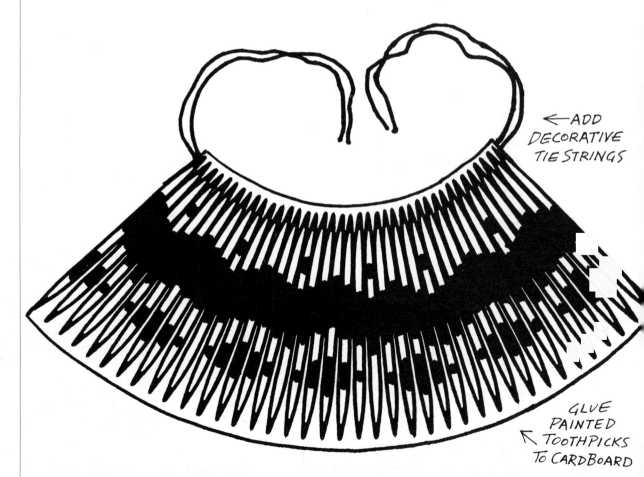

←ADD DECORATIVE TIE STRINGS

GLUE PAINTED TOOTHPICKS TO CARDBOARD

FAMILY LIFE

A female porcupine has just one young a year, and she raises it without any help from the male. The baby porky, called a *porcupette*, is quite good sized — about a pound at birth — and its eyes are open. It has soft quills when it's born, but the quills harden in just a few minutes. Then watch out, because those tiny quills are sharp and dangerous. Porcupettes can travel short distances right away but can't do much tree climbing for awhile, so the mother often leaves the porcupette tucked safely in a den during the day. Then she'll take it with her at night when she feeds.

IT'S MY TERRITORY

The males of most species fight over territory, but not the porcupine. It's the female porkies who stake out a territory and defend it against other females. The porcupine is an unusual animal in many ways, including this one!

LET'S TALK ABOUT IT

Porkies are fun to listen to. If you disturb one in its den, it may squeak, grumble, groan, and mutter to itself in ways that are apt to make a person laugh. Porkies also have a high-pitched cry that many people have mistakenly thought was the scream of a bobcat or mountain lion.

FUN FACTS

Fossils of porcupine ancestors date back about thirty million years (30,000,000), or about ten million years later than the earliest members of the weasel family. That's still a very, very long time, so porcupines have been successful at the most important thing of all — survival.

GRUMBLE! GROAN! MUTTER!

THE BEAVER

• RANGE MAP •

Have you ever heard the expression "busy as a beaver"? Beavers probably got that reputation because they can take down a large tree in just a few nights, and their dams seem to appear out of nowhere. Beavers certainly know how to gnaw! Their big front teeth are like sharp chisels, and they can take out a large chip of wood in a single bite.

The beaver is a member of a very large group of mammals (including mice and squirrels) called *rodents* that all have front teeth made for gnawing. The beaver is the second largest rodent in the world and sometimes weighs more than sixty pounds. Only the *capybara* (cap-ih-BAHR-ah), a rodent of South America, is bigger.

HOME
SWEET
HOME

Let's Build a Dam!

Beavers are famous for building dams, and they're amazingly good at it! Using their front paws, they pack mud, stones, sticks, and brush into a very strong, almost watertight, wall, or dam.

Behind the dam, water backs up and creates a pond so deep it won't freeze to the bottom in the winter! This way beavers can reach their food supply of branches stored at the bottom of the pond, even when the pond is frozen.

Do beavers always build dams? No, although they would if they could. Beavers that live in swift rivers and wide lakes where dams won't hold, often dig their homes in the banks. Some folks call them "bank beavers," but they're really just the same species of beaver adapting to their particular surroundings.

Like their dam, beavers use sticks and mud to build a house, or *lodge*, large enough to hold an entire beaver family. The lodge's floor is just above the water level, but tunnels in the lodge lead down to the deepest waters of the pond where winter food is stored and water cannot freeze.

Beavers are very safe in their lodge in the winter. The frozen walls are almost as strong as iron. Not even the strongest and hungriest wolf or mountain lion could dig its way in!

It's Great for Wildlife

Beaver ponds help other wildlife — ducks, herons, turtles, frogs, and fish — who feed, nest, or make the pond their home. When the beavers have used all the food around their pond, they move away. After a few years, the dam falls apart and the bottom of the pond becomes a *beaver meadow*. Grasses, shrubs, and other plants grow there and are important food for deer, moose, and other wildlife. Years later, when enough trees have grown back to provide food, other beavers will return and build another dam.

FAMILY LIFE

A beaver pond, along with the beavers living in it, is called a *colony* (a group of the same kind of creatures living close together). In beaver colonies, the beavers are all one family who share the work of repairing the dam and lodge and cutting down trees for food. They work mostly at night, and the parents are always alert for danger. Beavers are very protective of their territory. If a strange beaver tries to move in, the beavers will kill or drive away the intruder.

In the winter, the beaver family consists of the parents plus young beavers from the past two years. Then, in spring and early summer, after three or four new babies, or *kits*, are born, the two-year-old beavers must leave the colony to find a new home.

A pair of beavers will stay together for life, but if one dies, the other will find another mate. Several other wild creatures, such as the Canada goose and the wolf, do exactly the same thing.

Anyone Home?

See if you can find a beaver colony. This may not be as hard as you think, even if you live in a big city. Beavers can often be found surprisingly close to large cities. Your state or provincial wildlife agency, or a local conservation organization, may be able to tell you the location of a beaver colony.

Finding a beaver colony, dam, or lodge is one thing, but actually seeing the beavers is quite another. Beavers don't come out much in the daytime, so you may have to wait by a beaver pond at dusk or on a moonlit night in order to actually see a beaver.

Another way of finding beavers is to look for sticks that they've chewed the bark off. If these are fresh, they'll look almost white, and you can see that they've been bitten off at the ends. If you find fresh beaver cuttings along the banks of a stream, it means there are beavers somewhere upstream. If you find cuttings in a lake, then you can probably find a beaver lodge somewhere along the shoreline. (Be sure to stay away from the water's edge and never walk on an ice-covered pond, river, or lake.)

BUILD YOUR OWN BEAVER LODGE

Build two small beaver lodges. Make one out of modeling clay only. Shape it like a beaver lodge and then hollow out a room from the bottom. Now build another lodge, mixing plenty of toothpicks or small twigs, pointing in every direction, with the clay. Use plenty of sticks, and carefully work the clay in between the sticks. Think how a beaver lodge is made with sticks and mud, and try to make your second lodge that way. When you're done, remove enough clay and sticks from the bottom to make a room, just as you did with the first lodge.

Now put the two lodges side by side and push down on the top. Which lodge is stronger when you push on it? Does this tell you anything about why beavers use both sticks and mud to build their lodges? Do you know the story, *The Three Little Pigs?* Which little pig's house do you think was really the most like the beaver's house, and why?

To finish the clay and sticks lodge, use a shoe box as a base so that you can build the lodge above water level, and have tunnels going down to a pond (shallow cup). Decorate with branches, twigs, and other natural objects.

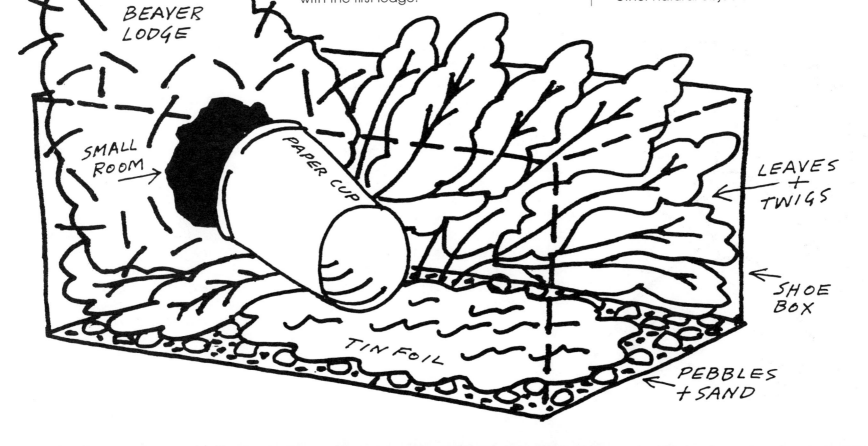

BEAVER LODGE

SMALL ROOM →

PAPER CUP

LEAVES + TWIGS

SHOE BOX

TIN FOIL

PEBBLES + SAND

NATIVE AMERICAN LEGENDS

Naturally Speaking

Beavers are right at home in the water and spend much of their time in it. They can stay underwater for at least 15 minutes without coming up for air, and their nose and ears have valves — a sort of plug to keep the water out when they dive. They also have special features in their mouth and throat to keep them from swallowing water while they work underwater. These are interesting physical, underwater *adaptations,* or special features, for mammals to have.

Beavers have large hind feet that are webbed, much like a duck's feet. These big, webbed feet make the beaver a very good swimmer and diver. As you've seen, the beaver needs all of these adaptations because of the way it lives.

Take a breath: There are two reasons why beavers can stay underwater so long. One is that their heart beat slows to half its normal rate when the beaver dives, so the beaver uses less oxygen underwater. The second reason is that beavers can use most of the oxygen (75 percent) in their lungs, while we humans can only use a small part (15 percent) of the oxygen in ours.

If you've ever had "the hiccups," then you've probably tried holding your breath for a while to get rid of them. Most people can hold their breath comfortably for only about 15 – 20 seconds. Try holding your breath for 15 seconds. Did it feel easy or difficult? Imagine holding it for 15 minutes like the beaver!

Animals were of the greatest importance to American Indians. The beaver was especially important because it was good to eat, and its beautiful fur provided fine, warm clothing. It's not surprising that animals were given credit in Native American legends for doing wonderful things.

Here is a legend from the Cree Indians near James Bay in Saskatchewan that makes the beaver a great hero and explains where he got his magnificent fur coat and sharp teeth.

The sun was too far away to give the earth enough heat, so the Great Spirit snared it and brought it closer. But then the sun was too close and too hot, and threatened to scorch the earth.

The sun said that if someone freed it, it would come to the edge of the earth in the morning and evening, but would stand overhead at noon. Now, it happened that all the other animals looked down on the lowly beaver; they also were afraid to go near the hot sun. But the beaver was brave and went to the sun and gnawed through the snare to set the sun free. All the beaver's hair was burned off, though. Then the Great Spirit rewarded the beaver for his bravery by giving him the finest of all animal coats, as well as big, strong teeth for cutting down trees.

An Amazing Tail!

Beavers have a very wide, flat, scaly tail which looks as if it would be useful for packing mud for a dam — but it isn't. In spite of that, the beaver's tail is quite amazing because it helps its owner in many other ways.

If a beaver senses danger, it slaps its tail on the water as a warning to the other beavers. The tail helps the beaver to steer from side to side — sort of like a rudder — when it's swimming at the surface of the water, and to go up and down when it's diving, much as diving planes on a submarine help it to dive or surface.

When the beaver sits on its haunches to gnaw on a tree, it uses that wide, flat tail as a brace to help it sit upright. The tail stores fat that the beaver can use if food becomes very scarce. Why, it even helps regulate the beaver's body temperature by passing heat into the water. You can see that the beaver's tail is like a whole tool kit, even if it isn't used to pack mud!

Custom-designed tails: Think about the different kinds of tails that birds and animals have. The beaver uses its tail for many things, but what are other kinds of tails good for? What about some common domestic animals, like cats, dogs, cows, and horses? Do they use their tails for anything? You should be able to figure out how some birds and animals use their tails, although others may not seem to have any particular use. If you were an animal, what kind of tail would you like to have, and why?

The Layered Look

Do you wear two coats at once? Beavers do — both of them are fur that contains oils that repel water. The glossy outer coat is made of *guard hairs*. Beneath this coat is the *underfur*, which is so thick that water can't even get to the beaver's skin! Is it any wonder that beavers can swim around under the ice and not freeze? This experiment shows you how the oil in a beaver's coat keeps the water away from its skin.

Here's what you'll need:

Drinking straw, small plate

Cold water

Vegetable oil

Using the straw as you would an eye-dropper, put a few drops of cold water on the plate. Then pick up a drop of vegetable oil with the straw and drop it on top of the water. What happens? Does the water separate from the oil?

WHAT'S FOR DINNER?

Although beavers spend most of their time in the water, they don't eat fish. The beaver's winter food supply consists of the inner bark and tips of tree branches. The ends of these branches are buried in the mud so that they'll stay underwater. When a beaver wants a meal, all it has to do is swim out of a tunnel, cut off a piece of a branch, and take it back into the lodge. There it can feast on the tender bark and buds. In summer, beavers also enjoy a variety of soft water plants growing in their pond.

FUN FACTS

Beavers are about three feet long, but there was a beaver called *Trogonotherium*, living about a million years ago, which was seven feet long. Early humans were around then, so they must have seen these monster beavers!

Down They Go

Beavers played a major part in the settlement of North America by Europeans. American Indians weren't the only ones who valued beaver fur to keep them warm and dry; beaver hats and coats were in great demand in Europe, so many early explorers went across North America trapping or trading for beaver skins with American Indians.

The white settlers cut down the forests on which the beavers depended, and there were few places for beavers to live. Also, there were no laws at all to control trapping. Then beavers became very scarce in most places.

And Back They Come!

Then, as the forests grew back and strict laws limited the number of beavers that could be trapped, the beavers returned. Today we have so many beavers that they're often a real nuisance. They block culverts, flood roads, and even come into people's yards to cut down fruit and shade trees. The beavers don't know any better, of course; to them, a narrow culvert is simply a good place to put a dam, and one tree is just like another.

Because beavers are big and strong, with very sharp teeth, not many animals can prey on them. Once wolves and mountain lions controlled the number of beavers, but these big predators don't mix well with humans and won't return to many of the areas where beavers live. Now humans are the main predator of beavers.

Find the Beaver

This puzzle has nine important words associated with beavers hidden within the letters. Copy the puzzle onto a piece of paper (don't write in your book) and try to find these hidden beaver words: beaver, dam, mate, lodge, rodent, colony, fur, kits, water. Do you know why each of these words is important to beavers?

Puzzle

```
k n y w f o d b r
x l m a t e b x s
p c a t q u e g t
r o d e n t a y i
s l h r i b v r k
t o l o d g e a s
w n c n f u r t z
h y u p r a k b o
```

THE GRAY AND THE RED SQUIRRELS

FOOD KEY

- NUTS
- MUSHROOMS
- BIRD EGGS
- MICE

• RANGE MAP •

- ▇ Gray Squirrel
- ▇ Red Squirrel
- ▇ Both Gray and Red Squirrels

There's a lot of misinformation about squirrels. One belief is that red squirrels drive out the grays, but that certainly isn't true. If they did, we wouldn't have gray squirrels in the many areas where both species live (see range map). Probably this myth started because red squirrels are quite aggressive about defending the territory around their dens. If another squirrel — red or gray — gets too close, the red will chase it away. However, if a red squirrel pursues a gray too closely, the much bigger gray will turn around and put the red in its place in a hurry! Actually, both red and gray squirrels often inhabit the same piece of woods and seldom bother each other.

LET'S TALK ABOUT IT

It's surprising how many people think gray squirrels are nice and yet they dislike red squirrels. There's no real reason for this; one isn't nicer than the other, although they're quite different in a number of ways. In fact, many people who are really familiar with squirrels think that reds are more interesting than grays. Perhaps it's the voice of the red squirrel that makes people think it is nasty, because one of the biggest differences between red and gray squirrels is in the sounds they make.

Gray squirrels don't make a lot of noise, but they have a kind of high, raspy bark. The noisy little red squirrels are nothing like their quieter cousins. Red squirrels are easily upset, and whenever one is disturbed it chirrs, squeaks, grunts, squabbles, chatters, and sputters like a tiny teakettle boiling over. All of this noise is accompanied by jerks of the tail, foot shuffling, and other head and body movements. No one ever accused red squirrels of being quiet! The red squirrel sound most easily heard for long distances is a long, drawn-out *chirrrrrrrrrr* that may last for ten seconds or more.

ACORN

BEECHNUT

PINECONE

MAPLE SEED

A WALK ON THE WILD SIDE

If you live in the city, you can probably watch gray squirrels, which are common in most city parks. If you have a bird feeder, grays will probably come to it, too — and so will reds if they live in your area. Try to go out in the woods, though, and watch squirrels in a natural setting. You'll probably have much better luck watching reds. Truly wild gray squirrels in the woods tend to be quite wary and hide as soon as they see a human. Reds are more apt to sit and scold you for long periods of time! Watching them is easy and a lot of fun.

Take a bag with you in the woods and pick up things a squirrel might eat, or the remains of things they've eaten. Look for nuts and large seeds, such as maple seeds, pinecones or pinecone scales left by red squirrels at a favorite feeding spot, or nuts with a hole gnawed in them. Try to identify all the different kinds of squirrel food you've found. Save them to make a seed and nut collage (see page 52).

When gray squirrels dig up nuts they've buried, they miss a lot of them. Some of the nuts left in the ground sprout and grow up to be nut trees. Black walnuts, butternuts, and hickories, especially, need squirrels to plant them, because they don't sprout very well on top of the ground. Some biologists think that at least nine out of every ten hickory and black walnut trees came from a nut buried by a squirrel. Nuts are very important to squirrels, but do you think squirrels are also very important to these nut trees?

Plant some nut trees: You'll need to find some nuts — acorns should work well — that have just fallen off the trees in autumn and haven't been eaten out by squirrels. Last year's seeds usually won't sprout. Plant each nut the way a gray squirrel does, in a hole about two inches deep. Then cover it with dirt and leave it for the winter. Be sure to mark where each nut is planted with a wooden stake or something else you can find easily in the spring. Some nuts won't sprout, and it may be early summer before other seedlings poke through the ground, so don't be too impatient. Your state forestry or conservation department may be able to give you other tips on how to plant nuts.

Nut Hunt

Is your memory or sense of smell as keen as a squirrel's? Have your own nut hunt and find out! Count out 20 nuts — unshelled peanuts will work fine — and bury them in secret hiding places in the house or outdoors. Wait 2 days. Then, try to find as many buried nuts as you can. Can you find them by sniffing? Can you find them by using other senses and being very observant (look for ground that has been disturbed recently). Imagine being able to smell the nuts under the ground like a squirrel — that's some sniffer! Now, count your nuts, and see how close you came to finding the 20 that were buried.

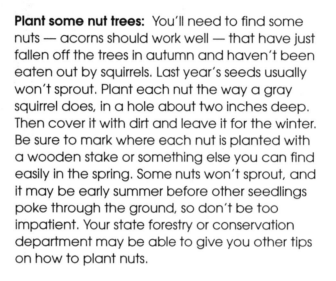

WHAT'S FOR DINNER?

Gray and red squirrels eat much the same things, with one big difference — red squirrels eat the seeds found inside pine, spruce, and balsam fir cones. Do you know how people look when they eat corn on the cob? Red squirrels look just like that when they feed on cones. The little squirrel sits up and holds one end of a cone with each front paw. Then it turns the cone while gnawing rapidly. The scales fly in every direction, and the squirrel eats each seed (one at the base of each scale) without seeming to pause in its chewing. It's quite a performance — one that's a lot of fun to watch!

Both gray and red squirrels eat nuts, seeds, mushrooms, and fruits, but grays depend much more heavily on nuts than reds do. In years when there are few nuts, many grays may starve during the winter. Both grays and reds sometimes become predators, too, and eat birds' eggs, baby birds, and young mice if they can find them.

HOME SWEET HOME

Both gray and red squirrels prefer a *cavity* (a deep hole) in a tree trunk for a den. In fact, a gray squirrel may have as many as seven different dens in trees and move often from one to another. It may be that they're trying to get away from the hordes of fleas that sometimes infest dens. Biologists have sometimes found thousands of fleas in one squirrel den. Wouldn't you move out of your room if you were being bitten by thousands of fleas? One biologist who was studying squirrels had to shave off his beard because so many fleas hopped into it!

Have you ever seen a big ball of leaves left high up in a tree after the leaves have fallen in the fall? If you have, you were probably looking at a gray squirrel's summer nest. When there aren't enough dens in tree trunks, gray squirrels often build these leaf nests. Red squirrels occasionally build leaf nests, too. But, if tree cavities are scarce, the red is more apt to dig a den underneath a tree or use a hollow log.

FAMILY LIFE

Like so many animals, male squirrels have nothing to do with raising their young, but the females are extremely good mothers who take excellent care of their babies. The little squirrels are naked, blind, and helpless at first, so they need a lot of care. Gray squirrels usually have two or three young in a litter, reds four or five. Farther south, both species sometimes have two litters a year, one in early spring and another in late summer.

Seed and Nut Collage

Collect as many kinds of seeds and nuts as you can find outside. Look on the ground, under trees and fallen leaves, and in the garden for acorns, hickory nuts, sunflower seeds, and maple tree seeds. Add things you found on your walk on the wild side (see page 49). If it is slim pickings outdoors, scout around your kitchen for store-bought nuts, seeds, and even dried beans. Sort them into small piles or in paper cups by type, by size, or by color. Create a picture with your seeds that reflects the season. Simply spread glue on posterboard or cardboard so that you have a shape (a squirrel, other wildlife, or a creative arrangement of colors and shapes) that captures your sense of the texture and colors available to you. Anything goes, so create your collage the way you would like to see it!

Gray squirrels usually spend the winter snug in a cavity in a big old tree. They're very social at that time of year, too. Several male squirrels will share the same den, as will young females. Older females spend the winter alone.

Red squirrels also like tree cavities, but they often winter in dens they've dug between the roots of trees, or even stay in tunnels in the snow. When they have snow tunnels, they'll pop up out of tunnel openings like a jack-in-the-box! Red squirrels always den alone, except for mothers with young.

Build a winter nesting box: It's often hard for squirrels, especially grays, to find enough cavities in trees for winter quarters. If you live where there are gray squirrels, build a nesting box for them (you can do this for reds, too, if you wish — they can always use a winter home, too). You'll need help from a grown-up in making and putting up the box. You can get plans for a nesting box by writing for *Woodworking for Wildlife* from Pennsylvania Game Commission, Dept. MS, 2001 Elmerton Ave., Harrisburg, PA 17110-9797. The cost is $3.00 (plus a 6% tax for Pennsylvania residents).

Where's the Pantry?

Do you know what a pantry is? Almost every house used to have a pantry — a place to store food — although most newer houses no longer have one. Both red and gray squirrels have a sort of pantry, but they're quite different for each species. Grays, as you already know, bury nuts one by one and then find them by smell. Reds, on the other hand, usually store food in a large *cache* (a hiding place for safe keeping) underground or in a hollow tree. The U.S. Forest Service has found that the very best source of seeds for planting coniferous trees is a red squirrel's storehouse. When a forester finds a seed cache, he or she takes the seeds for planting and replaces them with grain or other seeds so that the squirrel doesn't starve.

Where's the Dining Room?

Lots of homes have a dining room or dining area. Do you have a particular place where you usually eat? Red squirrels do; they usually have a favorite feeding stump or log and soon accumulate a big pile of cone scales and empty nut shells. Some of these piles are large enough to fill a bushel basket. It's hard to imagine that such a small animal caused such a great heap of cone scales!

The Nose Knows

In the fall, when nuts are plentiful, gray squirrels regularly bury them. Because the squirrels find many of the buried nuts, people believe the squirrels "remember" where they bury each nut. Gray squirrels do seem to sense the general area where they've buried nuts, but biologists have learned that they find the exact location of a nut by scent. They can even smell a buried nut through many inches of snow. Do you think you could find your food buried underground beneath deep snow?

Gray squirrels use this very good sense of smell in another way, too. Biologists have found that if they touch baby gray squirrels in a den, the mother will move the babies to another den right away. Apparently she smells the human scent and thinks that a strange scent may mean danger to her young.

THE RED FOX

FOOD KEY

MICE

GRASSHOPPER

BIRDS' EGGS

BERRIES

RABBIT

• RANGE MAP •

It's always easy to think wild animals are bigger than they really are, and that's especially true of foxes. Most people seem to think that a fox weighs about as much as a medium-small dog, but it really only weighs about as much as a house cat. Do you or your neighbors have a cat? If so, how much does it weigh? (Look on page 29 to learn how to weigh a cat on your home scales.)

An average red fox weighs about ten pounds. If a fox weighs so little, why does it appear to be so much bigger? It's because of its long legs, thick fur, and beautiful tail, which is called a *brush*. That handsome brush, which looks so big and full, actually weighs almost nothing and just seems to float along behind the fox. Underneath all that fur, the fox has a very skinny body, and that's one reason it can run so fast!

The wolf and the red fox both belong to the dog family, but they're very different in many ways, such as the way they hunt. The fox, as you will see, actually has a lot of catlike qualities.

Native to North America?

For a long time scientists argued about whether the red fox was native to North America or whether it was introduced to North America by English settlers who brought red foxes to the southern United States for their favored pastime — fox hunting on horseback. Scientists have now found red fox fossils and bones that date from before Columbus came to the New World (long before the English settlers, of course).

Red foxes weren't nearly as common then as they are now. The smaller gray fox probably greatly outnumbered the red fox in the days before the European settlers arrived. Why? Because gray foxes are a forest animal, while red foxes do best around fields, brush areas, and the edges of woods. How do you think the coming of the European settlers helped the red fox?

As you can see from the range map at the top of page 54, the red fox is found almost everywhere in North America now. That means you have a good chance of seeing one of these interesting, beautiful animals with their bright orange-red coat and black legs that look as if they are wearing black stockings.

■

A WALK ON THE WILD SIDE

Winter, after a fresh snow, is a good time to find fox tracks. Look in fields, pastures, and brush areas for footprints that look like the tracks of a very small, light-weight dog. Study the fox tracks around this page to help you in accurate identification. If you find fox tracks in February, you may notice a strong, skunk odor. That's because the male fox's urine takes on that strong smell during its mating season, which begins about the end of January.

It's OUR Territory!

A pair of foxes has a territory, but it's nowhere near as big as the territory of a pack of wolves. The dog fox marks his territory with urine, much like the alpha male wolf. Foxes defend their territory against other foxes, but they probably don't kill each other in disputes over territory the way wolves do.

WHAT'S FOR DINNER?

Foxes eat many things, including birds' eggs, berries, nuts, and a lot of meat. They catch prey as large as rabbits and hares or as small as insects. However, foxes are especially good at catching mice, voles, and other small rodents, and each fox hunts alone — much more like a cat than like wolves and other members of the dog family.

Have you ever seen a cat stalk a mouse and pounce on it? If you have, have you seen the cat play with the mouse before killing and eating it? Well, foxes hunt in almost the same way.

Fun Reads

Flossie & the Fox
by Patricia C. McKissack

Fantastic Mr. Fox
by Roald Dahl

Mother West Wind's Children
by Thornton W. Burgess

FUN FACTS

Both the dog and cat families evolved from a common ancestor — a group called *miacids.* Miacids were rather small, weasel-like predators, and dogs and cats began to evolve from them about 40 million years ago. That's about 25 million years after the dinosaurs became extinct.

Stalk and pounce: The fox sneaks along until it hears the rustle of a mouse or vole in the grass. Then it turns its head from side to side, using its wonderful ears to figure out the exact location of its prey. The fox will *stalk* its prey and then *pounce* on it. You can find the word stalk in the dictionary and discover that it has several meanings. One meaning is to *walk softly.* Try stalking as if you were a hunting fox; then, *pounce!* How is pouncing different than jumping? What part of your body helps you pounce? The fox leaps high in the air and comes almost straight down, its front legs extended to pin the mouse beneath its front feet. Where do you think the fox must have strong muscles?

NATIVE AMERICAN LEGENDS

The red fox is the only wild member of the dog family in North America that has a white tip on its tail. The members of the Acoma Pueblo in New Mexico explained this with a fun myth.

■

Once, while the fox was fast asleep, the mice nibbled all the fur from its tail to make a soft, warm bed for themselves. But the fox woke up when the mice bit the end of its tail, and it chased the mice away.

The fox put all the fur in a pile. Then it put pitch from the pinon (PIN-yon) pine on its tail and rolled its tail in the pile of fur. The sticky pitch held the fur so that it was thick and tight on the tail — but the mice had "eaten" all the color out of the fur that was now back at the tip of the fox's tail!

■

FAMILY LIFE

There are usually five or six pups born in one of the fox's dens, though there may be as many as nine, and some of the smaller, weaker ones usually die. The female fox, called a *vixen*, stays with the pups all the time for nearly two weeks, probably to keep them warm. Like the male wolf, the male fox (called the *dog fox*) brings food to the vixen while she stays in the den. Later, they both bring food to the pups.

When the pups are about a month old, they begin to fight with each other. The biggest, strongest pup quickly becomes the alpha (see page 103), and the others find their own social level, down to the weakest pup. This seems like a wolf family, except that foxes don't live in packs. The pups are nearly full grown by fall and go off on

their own, leaving the male and female fox to raise another litter the next spring.

Weigh in: A newborn fox — called a pup, kit, or cub — weighs about a quarter of a pound, the same as one stick of margarine. Hold a stick of margarine in your hand and imagine you are holding a fox kit.

Ask a parent how much you weighed when you were born. You probably weighed several *pounds*. There are four 1/4-pound sticks in a box of margarine — four sticks weigh 1 pound ($4 \times \frac{1}{4} = 1$). How many sticks of margarine would you need to weigh as many pounds as you did at birth? How many 1-pound boxes of margarine?

The average adult red fox weighs about 10 pounds. That would be 10 boxes of margarine.

★ Fox and Mouse Game ★

A fox is able to hear the rustle of a mouse or a vole in the grass. That's wonderful hearing! The fox turns from side to side to determine the exact location of its prey. How well do your ears work at helping you locate sounds? You can play a game of **Fox and Mouse** to test your hearing. This game can be played with four or more friends — the more players, the more difficult.

Choose one person to be the "fox." The other players are mice; they form a circle around the "fox" who stands in the center with eyes closed. One "mouse"

enters the circle, walks around the fox, and returns to the same spot in the circle. All the children call out, "Foxy, foxy, where am I?" The "fox" must point to the child who was the "mouse." If "fox" guesses correctly, then the "mouse" and "fox" trade places, and the game continues with a new "fox."

Now that you've tried listening like a fox, what did you discover about using your ears? Did you turn your head as a fox does? How did you determine the location of the "mouse"?

Foxes don't howl, but they make quite a few different noises. Many of these are more catlike than doglike. One sound is a short, mewing cry — a sort of high-pitched "yaaah, yaaah." When they're alarmed, foxes give a kind of high scream, and they also have a short, yappy bark.

That wily old fox: Although the fox may not make very distinctive sounds, it certainly has given us a lot to talk about. There are all sorts of expressions that have to do with being "foxy" or sneaky, or wily, or sly, like the fox in *The Gingerbread Man.* Can you think of other words to describe a fox?

The fox's character is so much a part of our folklore that there are even songs about it. Here are the first two verses of a well-known folk song about a fox out hunting at night — and all the mischief he gets into. See if you can make up a few more verses about his adventures (notice that lines 4 and 6 repeat with slight variations in each verse). You can find the tune in a book of folk songs.

The fox went out on a chilly night,
And prayed for the moon to give him light.
He had many a mile to go that night,
Before he reached the town oh, town oh, town oh,
He had many a mile to go that night,
Before he reached the town oh.

He ran 'til he came to a great big pen.
The ducks and the geese were kept therein.
"A couple of you will grease my chin,
Before I leave this town oh, town oh, town oh,
A couple of you will grease my chin,
Before I leave this town oh."

Foxes have evolved to be like cats in many ways, and that's why they hunt like cats. Cats try to sneak up on their prey and pounce on it, and, unlike wolves, so do foxes. Cats can *retract* (pull in) their claws, and foxes can retract their claws part way. This helps them move quietly, so they can sneak close to their prey. Foxes also arch their backs and walk sideways, almost like a cat, when they're angry or upset.

Have you ever noticed how a cat's eyes change in different light? In bright sunlight, the *pupil* (the dark part in the center of the eye) is just a narrow slit pointed up and down. When there's very little light, the cat's pupils become big and round. The fox has exactly the same type of eyes so that, like the cat, it can see very well in either bright or dim light.

Night vision: Here's a way for you and a friend to experiment with the effect of light on the eye's pupil. Ask a friend to stand near a window and look out into the light. Look at the pupils of his eyes. Now have him shut out the light by keeping his eyes open but covering them with his clean hands. Count to ten, then have him uncover his eyes. What did the pupils do? They act like a window, adjusting to allow just the right amount of light through, closing in bright light and opening wide in low light. The pupil of a fox's eye is even more sensitive to changes in light than the human eye. This enables the fox to hunt its prey in dim light.

THE WEASEL FAMILY

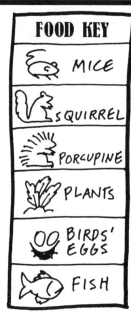

FOOD KEY

MICE

SQUIRREL

PORCUPINE

PLANTS

BIRDS' EGGS

FISH

A skunk is a *weasel*? Well, not exactly, but it's a member of the weasel *family*, which makes it a close relative. But how can that be? How can the roly-poly, slow-moving skunk be closely related to the swift, slender little weasel?

Just as in human families, looks, and even names, are often deceiving. Do all of your cousins share the same last name that you have? Well, the weasel family doesn't always share the same name, but the members of the weasel family do share a couple of traits that make them related.

First, the weasel family members have scent glands under the base of the tail; although only skunks can spray their scent for a distance, the scent of the others is strong, musky, and unpleasant.

Second, weasel family members, except for the *least weasel*, have the same sort of system that bears have; after mating, the tiny, fertilized egg usually doesn't start to grow for awhile, sometimes for weeks or months.

But the most wonderful thing about the weasel family is the way different members have adapted themselves to almost every kind of habitat, from the *marten* in the tree tops to the *badger* underground to the *otter* underwater. Probably no other family of mammals has managed to use so many kinds of habitat so well.

The striped skunk, otter, and mink live in almost all regions of North America. Only in the southernmost reaches of the U.S. are the otter and mink uncommon. The badger's range extends from the midwestern regions of the U.S. to California, and up through the midwestern provinces of Canada. The ermine and least weasel live in the colder, northern regions of North America. The long-tailed weasel is common in the southern reaches of the Canadian provinces, and in most of the U.S., with the exception of some southwest regions.

WEASELS

WHAT'S FOR DINNER?

Weasels are like other predators and kill in order to survive — not because they enjoy killing. Weasels burn food so fast that they have to eat about half their weight in food every day in order to survive. How much would you have to eat in order to do that? That's why weasels kill more than they can eat and store it in a *cache*, or storage place — sometimes as many as thirty or forty mice at a time. It's a lot like humans who stock up on groceries when they hear a big storm is coming.

Although weasels can climb trees, they spend most of their lives on the ground, racing about searching for enough prey to keep them alive. All weasels are great mousers, but the least weasel — the smallest true *carnivore* (meat-only eater) in the world — lives almost entirely on mice. The ermine and long-tailed weasel also kill larger prey, such as squirrels, chipmunks, rabbits, and occasionally a farmer's hens.

Have you ever seen a weasel? If you have, you aren't likely to forget this quick, darting little animal with its bright, beady eyes! There are three kinds of weasels in North America. The smallest is the *least weasel* (7" – 8"long, weight about 2 ounces), the largest is the *long-tailed weasel* (17" long, weight about 10 ounces), and the in-between size is the *ermine* or *short-tailed weasel.*

LEAST WEASEL → 8"

ERMINE → 10"

LONG-TAILED WEASEL → 17"

Nature's Winter Coat

Have you ever seen a very strange sight — a black dot that seems to move across the winter snow? If you have, you were probably watching an ermine, or a long-tailed weasel. Weasels are brown in summer, but in winter in the north they turn white. The least weasel becomes completely white, but the other two keep a black tip on their tails. Turning white in winter *camouflages* the weasel and lets it get closer to its prey. The black tip on the tail may cause larger predators to attack the tip of the weasel's tail instead of its whole body. This is a fine example of how animals have evolved to protect themselves. Look at the section on polar bears on page 95. Do you see any similarities?

THE MARTEN

The marten looks like a big weasel (about two feet long) with beautiful brown fur and a tail that's a little bushier, but it usually weighs less than two and a half pounds. It would take four martens to weigh about as much as an average house cat.

Martens are called *arboreal* which means they're very much at home in the trees. They're so good at climbing and running around in tree tops that they often catch squirrels in the trees — and that's not easy to do! They also spend a lot of time on the ground, where they eat mice, voles, hares, birds, eggs, and dead animals.

BADGER
SKUNK
FISHER
MINK
MARTEN
OTTER

If you could choose: Think how each member of the weasel family lives. If you were an animal, which one would you like to be? Why?

WHAT'S FOR DINNER?

THE FISHER

Porcupine's for dinner, that's what — at least as often as a fisher can find one. The fisher is the only major predator of porcupines, and it kills them whenever it can. Fishers can move tremendously fast, and they dart in and out and bite the porcupine around the face, where it has no quills. Sometimes the fisher gets a face full of quills, and a few fishers die from it, but most of the time the fisher is too quick for the porky. Fishers eat lots of other things, too — hares, grouse, mice, birds, berries, nuts, and dead animals.

The fisher looks a lot like a marten, only it's a lot bigger. A really large male can weigh 15 to 18 pounds or so — bigger than most house cats — but the average is smaller. Females are only about half the size of males. The fisher has a beautiful, glossy coat so dark brown that it looks almost black at a distance. It also has a nice, bushy tail that makes it look bigger than it really is.

What's in a Name?

People often wrongly call the fisher a *fisher cat.* The fisher is a member of the weasel family and isn't related to cats at all — and in spite of its name, it doesn't catch fish.

Express yourself!: Have you ever noticed that some people have curious expressions and sayings? Maybe you've heard someone in your family say that you were "busy as a beaver," or "sly as a fox." Have you ever "weaseled out of something"? These sayings were made up based on people's impressions of wildlife.

Beavers really are busy creatures, building dams and lodges, and cutting down trees. And foxes are sly, too — often so swift and cunning that it's very hard for other animals to catch them.

Some sayings are just based on misunderstandings about wild creatures. For instance, the expression that someone is "blind as a bat" is misleading. Bats aren't blind; they just don't see as well as they use their "radar."

Can you think of any other expressions about animals? What about one based on another weasel; have you ever been accused of "badgering" (pestering) your brother or sister? Read page 67 and see if you can figure out how the badger got that expression?

THE OTTER

Everyone seems to love otters, perhaps because they often seem very playful with their amusing, whiskery faces. Whatever the reason, the otter seems to be people's favorite member of the weasel family.

Otters have short fur, long, tapered tails, and look very sleek. They are one of the largest members of the weasel clan, sometimes measuring four and a half feet long and weighing as much as thirty-three pounds. Although that's not very big compared with some animals, it's plenty big enough for the otter to take care of itself against most predators. Many a large dog has found that a much smaller otter, with its mouth full of sharp teeth, is more than a match!

Gone Fishin'

Because otters swim so swiftly, they can catch fish, so that's what they often dine on. But they also eat frogs, crayfish, salamanders, snakes, mice, and other small mammals.

Water Lovers

Otters are *aquatic*, which means they spend much of their time in the water. Like seals in the ocean, otters dive, roll, and play as easily as you might play tag on a playground. Otters don't just stay in the water, though. Males, in particular, will wander for miles across land, travelling from one body of water to another, or just looking for food.

Web-footed wonders: If you've ever worn flippers or fins on your feet while swimming, then you know how they help you move quickly through the water. Otters have big, webbed hind feet, almost like flippers, that propel them swiftly through the water.

You can see for yourself how their feet work — and you won't need flippers or a pool to do it! Next time you're in the bathtub, hold your fingers apart and push the water with your hands. Then, move your fingers so there is no space between them. Now push the water with your hands. Were you able to push more water with your fingers close together or opened? Now you can see why otters are such good swimmers.

Slipping and Sliding

Have you ever been on a water slide? Was it fun? Otters love to slide, too. They'll find a slippery mud bank, or a steep, snowy bank above open water in the winter, and slide down it over and over. Even when it's travelling in the snow, an otter will slide every chance it gets. Whenever it finds even a gentle slope, it tucks its front legs underneath, pushes hard with its hind legs, and toboggans along as far as it can.

THE MINK

The mink is about the same size as the marten (see page 62), but it is darker, and its tail isn't as bushy. The mink's habits are about half way between those of the otter and the weasel. Like the otter, the mink is an expert swimmer and can catch fish. Like the weasel, the mink is a swift traveller on land and spends far more time there than the otter does. Besides fish, the mink also preys on frogs, crayfish, salamanders, muskrats, mice, voles, rabbits, and small birds.

Weasel Family Neighborhood

The weasel family is so large that their needs may be quite different, even though they live in the same neighborhood. You can make an exciting map of their family neighborhood on a large piece of butcher paper or poster board. Use glue with scraps of colored paper to create the habitat. Draw the animals or cut pictures from magazines.

1. Make a list of all the members of the weasel family.

2. Consider what each one needs for food, water, shelter, and space to grow.

3. Colored markers/crayons could mark each one's travels in the course of the day or night to get food and water and to return home safely. Have fun!

SKUNKS

Whew! A Skunk!

Have you ever seen or smelled a skunk? Almost every one has, because skunks are very common. Their strong, long-lasting scent certainly helps to repel most predators.

When we think of skunks, we usually think of the *striped skunk* that weighs up to 14 pounds, the size of a house cat. This black animal with the white stripes on its back is a familiar sight throughout most of North America. Sometimes its stripes are so wide that they come together, and its whole back is white. But there are other skunks in North America, including the *spotted skunk* — only weighing about a pound — which is also widespread and common.

Most members of the weasel family are active all winter, but not the skunk — at least not in cold northern areas. Although the skunk doesn't hibernate, it will take to its den when cold and snow arrive and stay there for weeks until the weather warms.

WHAT'S FOR DINNER?

Like opossums and raccoons, skunks will devour almost anything. They feed on earthworms, insects, nuts, garbage, dead animals, grain, mice, eggs, berries — just about everything an animal could possibly eat!

Skunks aren't quick to spray their scent; they only do it if they're frightened or feel very threatened. The striped skunk simply lifts its tail and sprays when danger threatens, but the spotted skunk has a very odd way of defending itself; it stands on its front feet when it sprays its scent. Skunks can spray scent for about twelve feet. A skunk can fire two or three full blasts of spray in quick succession if it has to. Then it has to recharge its scent glands — but that's not much help, because this only takes about half an hour!

It's hard to tell how the story got started that a skunk can't spray if it's picked up by the tail. People who have tried it have found out to their sorrow that it isn't true! Baby skunks are very cute, and people sometimes think it's safe to pick them up. It isn't, for two reasons. First, a baby skunk can spray its powerful scent when it's less than four weeks old, so watch out! If you don't want to smell like a skunk yourself, it's best to leave ALL skunks alone. Second, skunks can carry rabies, so it's not safe to handle them at any age, ever.

THE BADGER

Dig for Shelter and Food

Badgers are creatures of prairies, grasslands, and deserts. And where do they spend much of their time? In an underground den, of course. How would you like to live in a different home every day? Except for a female with young, a badger doesn't even bother to go back to the burrow it dug the day before; it just digs a new one!

Badgers are such great diggers that their main food supply consists of small rodents, such as prairie dogs, gophers, ground squirrels, and mice. When a badger finds a burrow with one of these inside, it simply outdigs its prey! They also eat frogs, crayfish, lizards, snakes, eggs, young birds, and even fox and coyote pups.

Badgers are one of the larger members of the weasel family, sometimes two and a half feet long and twenty-five pounds or more. With its sharp teeth, huge front claws, and great courage, a badger is nothing that most animals, even large ones, want to tackle.

The badger is helped greatly in a fight by its very loose skin, that makes it difficult for a predator to get a killing grip. If an animal seizes a badger by the neck, the badger wiggles around in its loose skin and bites its attacker savagely. How's that for an interesting adaptation?

If other members of the weasel family have taken to habitats in the trees or underwater, the badger has gone in a different direction — straight underground. This rather odd, flat-looking animal with black and white markings on its face is nature's steam shovel, a sort of live digging machine. With its tremendously long, strong front claws, a badger can dig in soft ground with almost unbelievable speed. The badger has a transparent inner eyelid that it lowers when it's digging. This keeps dirt out of its eyes but still allows the badger to see.

A WALK ON THE WILD SIDE

Look for tracks of members of the weasel family. In the winter, you may be able to find weasel, marten, or fisher tracks in the snow. Muddy places along lakes or streams are good places to look for otter or mink tracks. The tracks on the borders of these pages along with a good book on animal tracks will help tell you which tracks belong to weasel family members.

All members of the weasel family use dens at one time or another. Walk in the woods and along the edges of streams and ponds. How many different places can you find where a weasel, mink, marten, fisher, or otter might den? Think about the food they like and how they like to hunt to help you in your search.

Keeping Them Straight

With all of the members of the wonderful weasel family you may be having some difficulty keeping them straight! No wonder — it can seem pretty confusing at first. There are a lot of ways for you to organize this information. Here are some suggestions:

★ You could draw a chart (see page 130) to help you organize the information.

★ You might want to draw a bar graph to easily compare the weights or length of each kind of weasel (see page 99).

★ Perhaps you would like to make a drawing of each type of weasel and color it in. Or, if you like to work with modeling clay, make some action figures of the weasels in motion.

★ Do you like to write poems? A funny poem about the different weasels will certainly get you remembering and laughing.

★ Make some match-up cards (see page 37) that will provide a lot of fun and an easy way to learn which weasels do what.

★ And don't forget, you always have the option of remembering most about the weasel that interests you the most. That's usually the best method of all!

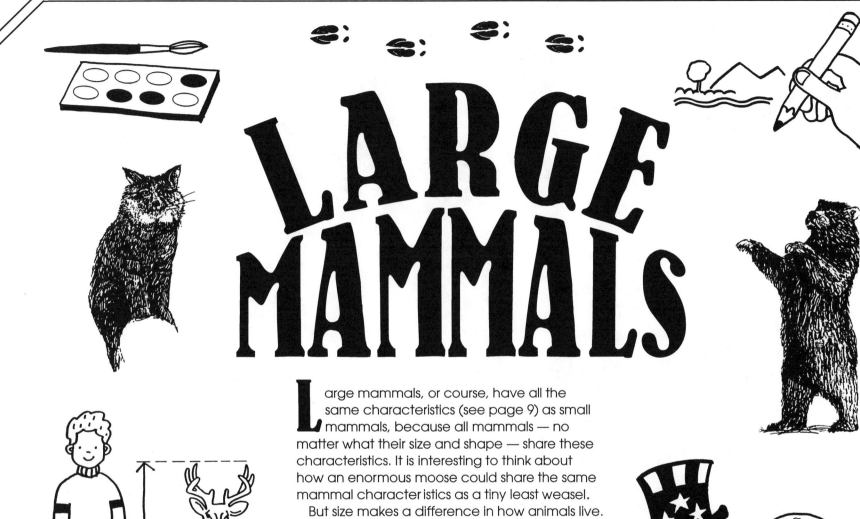

LARGE MAMMALS

Large mammals, or course, have all the same characteristics (see page 9) as small mammals, because all mammals — no matter what their size and shape — share these characteristics. It is interesting to think about how an enormous moose could share the same mammal characteristics as a tiny least weasel.

But size makes a difference in how animals live. See how many ways you and your friends and family can think of that large animals differ from small mammals. Would you rather be a small mammal or a very large one?

BOBCAT TRACK

THE WHITE-TAILED DEER

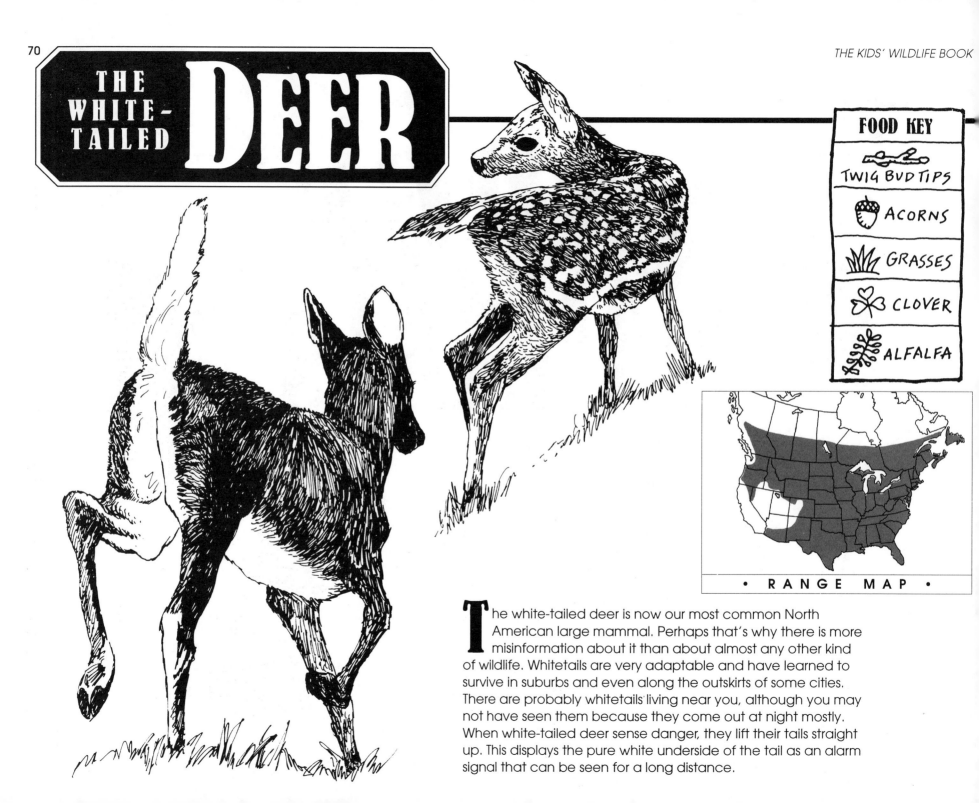

FOOD KEY

- TWIG BUD TIPS
- ACORNS
- GRASSES
- CLOVER
- ALFALFA

• RANGE MAP •

The white-tailed deer is now our most common North American large mammal. Perhaps that's why there is more misinformation about it than about almost any other kind of wildlife. Whitetails are very adaptable and have learned to survive in suburbs and even along the outskirts of some cities. There are probably whitetails living near you, although you may not have seen them because they come out at night mostly. When white-tailed deer sense danger, they lift their tails straight up. This displays the pure white underside of the tail as an alarm signal that can be seen for a long distance.

HOME SWEET HOME

White-tailed deer live in many kinds of habitat, but their favorite is a mix of forest, brush, swamps, and farmland. This kind of habitat gives them everything they need — a variety of food at different times of the year, shelter from snow and cold, and plenty of places to hide.

Deer don't defend their territory the way wolves and some other animals do, except for bucks during the fall mating season, or *rut.* Then, the bucks fight by clashing their antlers together and try to shove each other around. The winner, or *dominant buck,* then claims the territory and mates with the does. (He's a lot like the alpha male wolf, except that the alpha male is the boss all year, and not just in the mating season.)

FAMILY LIFE

Have you ever seen a very young fawn? Newborn fawns are about the same size as a newborn human baby, weighing only six or seven pounds. They have spots on their sides and backs that help them to hide from predators by blending into the grass and leaves.

Young fawns have very little scent, and this also helps to keep them safe from predators. The mother, or *doe,* will leave her fawns hidden for several hours at a time while she goes off to feed. By four months, the fawns have stopped nursing, have lost their spots, and look much like an adult deer. By November at about six months old, fawns usually weigh from 65 – 90 pounds and are ready for life on their own, although they may stay with their mother through the winter.

Fawn art: There is nothing more beautiful than a fawn in tall strands of grass. Why don't you draw a fawn, naturally camouflaged in real grass?

Here's what you'll need:

Piece of white paper, about 8½ x 11, or larger
Crayons, or water colors and paintbrush
Cotton balls
Pieces of tall grass or hay
Glue or paste, newspaper, pencil

Cover your work area with newspaper. Spread out your white paper. Sketch in the shape of your fawn — either standing or sitting in the grass. Draw it large so it fills the paper. Color your fawn a pale brown or paint it in water colors (let water colors dry before next step). Now, glue on some cotton balls for spots on the fawn's sides. Color in some green/brown grass and some pale blue sky. Then, glue on some real grass around the fawn. Ask if you can hang your fawn art on the refrigerator.

Popular Misunderstandings

Every year, people find tiny fawns that they think are orphans, and they take them home to raise as pets. This is a terrible mistake (and it's also against the law in most states). As you know now, usually the fawn isn't an orphan at all; its mother may be out feeding, or is hiding nearby. She'll be back soon to care for her baby, so leave the fawn where it is. (Some people believe that a doe will abandon her fawn if she smells human scent on it. It's absolutely untrue!)

It's not safe to keep a deer as a pet. Despite their great beauty and gentle appearance, deer are wild animals that are dangerous and unpredictable.

Prance and Dance

Deer are one of Mother Nature's most elegant creatures. These natural dancers leap, bound, and step with grace through forests and fields, often making little sound at all. Plus, they're *unguligrade*, which means they walk on their hoofs (which are really toes)!

Why not create a wonderful, one-of-a-kind, make-it-up-as-you-go-along deer dance as a tribute to this animal's natural beauty and grace! Create a style that's all your own, whether barefoot in the backyard or on your tippy toes in the living room. Keep in mind how deer react in certain situations. They can move slowly when cautious or calm; bound, leap, and generally prance when excited or frightened; and stand perfectly still and silent when trying to blend in with their surroundings.

FUN FACTS

No one knows just how many million whitetails there were in North America before the European settlers arrived. By the 1850s, however, there were fewer than one million left because of cutting down the forests (leaving fewer good wintering areas) and the lack of any laws to regulate hunting. But deer have increased rapidly, especially during the last few years. That's because much good habitat has grown back to forests and brush, and because strict laws control hunting. Biologists estimate there are now about 27 million whitetails in North America. That's quite a comeback!

THE WHITE-TAILED DEER • 73

POINTS

RACK

— BUCK —
(NINE
POINTER)

Horns and Antlers: What's the Difference?

Do you know the difference between horns and antlers? If you do, you know more than a lot of people, who often confuse the two. *Horns* are hollow; they don't branch, and an animal grows just one set of them in a lifetime. Cows, sheep, goats, bison, and musk oxen have horns.

Antlers are solid; they have branches and are shed each year during the winter. Then the animal grows a new set, starting in spring or early summer. At first, the new antlers are quite tender and have a soft, velvety covering. At this stage, antlers are said to be *in the velvet.* By early fall, the male deer's, or buck's, antlers have hardened, and he rubs them against saplings and small trees to remove the velvety covering. Deer, elk, moose, and caribou all have antlers, rather than horns.

A buck's antlers are called a *rack.* Each branch of its antlers is called a *point,* and a buck with four points on each side, for example, is said to be an *eight pointer* or have an *eight-point rack.* But you can't tell a buck's age by the size of its rack or the number of points on it. It's true that a buck usually grows larger antlers each year for its first four or five years, but many things besides age can affect antler size. The health of the buck, its winter food supply, and even the minerals in the soil can make a big difference. Biologists prefer to tell a deer's age from its teeth, because that's a much more accurate method.

NATIVE AMERICAN LEGENDS

How the Deer Got Its Antlers

The Cherokee of what is now Tennessee and North Carolina told this Native American tale to explain how the deer got its antlers.

■

The deer and the rabbit planned a race to see who was faster. It was supposed to be a fair contest, but the rabbit wanted to win so badly that it cheated by preparing a path through the brush and tall grass. Unbeknown to the rabbit, however, the owl was watching and saw him cheat. When the owl told the other animals, they awarded the prize — a fine set of antlers — to the deer before the race had even started. And thus the deer has always worn its majestic antlers.

■

Shadow play: Use your hands' shadows to act out an animal tale in your living room. Shadow a deer and a rabbit by simply shaping your hands in front of a bright light such as a flashlight or a bare lightbulb. (Don't touch the bulb; it gets very hot.) Your hands will cast a shadow on the wall. To make a rack of antlers, hold your hands as shown. Can you create a bunny with its ears? What about an owl or a bird flying overhead? Try telling the story as you act it out with hand shadows. Then ask someone else to make up a folk tale and do a shadow play, or just take turns creating shadows and guessing what they are.

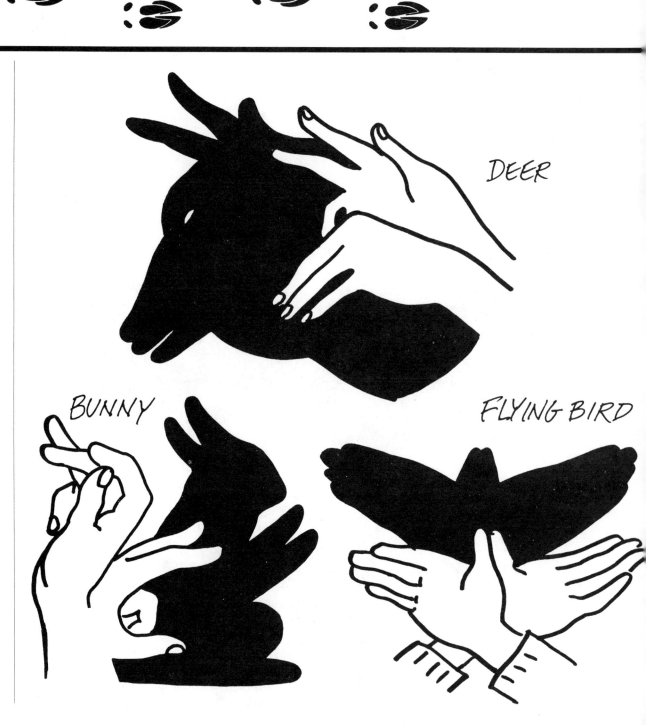

DEER

BUNNY

FLYING BIRD

Food for Thought

When warm weather foods — like grasses and mushrooms — are no longer around, deer eat different foods, mostly *browse*, or the tender tips of twigs. In the fall, acorns and beechnuts are an important part of their diet; they help build up body fat needed to survive especially cold, hard winters.

Have you ever heard of anyone in your area trying to feed deer during a very hard winter? Well-meaning people often try to give deer hay or grain when the deer are in danger of starving. Unfortunately, it doesn't help, and can harm the deer. Deer depend on bacteria and other tiny organisms (called *microorganisms*) in their stomachs to digest their food, and these microorganisms change according to the deer's seasonal diet. In the winter, when deer feed on browse, the microorganisms in their stomachs can't digest things like hay and grain. That's why deer can starve to death in the winter even with stomachs full of hay and grain!

WHERE SHALL WE SPEND THE WINTER?

A good deer wintering area (sometimes called a *deer-yard*, although nothing like a barnyard) has dense groves of tall *conifers* — at least 35 feet tall. The thick tops of the conifers (evergreens that have needles and cones) catch much of the snow, keep it from reaching the ground, and also help to break the wind. With less snow on the ground, it's much easier for the deer to make trails and move around to seek food. Good wintering areas are very important to the survival of deer in severe northern winters.

Environmentally yours: Find out from your local conservation officer where there are deer wintering areas near you, and then stay out of them in the winter. Urge others to stay out of them, too. Why? Because if deer are disturbed by humans or by dogs, they burn a great deal more energy running away than they would otherwise. In a severe winter, deer can die because of this extra energy loss!

How Big is BiG

Can you guess how tall an adult deer is? Most people guess way too high! A full-grown deer is only a little over three feet tall at the shoulder. Is that as tall as you are? Most bucks weigh less than 200 pounds, and the does weigh even less.

There's one very interesting thing about the size of deer; the farther north the deer live, the larger they're apt to be. There's a good reason for this: In cold weather, a large animal loses heat more slowly than a small one. That's because large animals have less surface area (the part of the animal that you can see) in relation to their weight. This is a great advantage for a larger animal in bitter winter weather farther north.

Keeping warm: Here's a way for you to understand why northern deer are larger than southern deer. Ask a grown-up to heat a pot of water to about 120 degrees or more. Then fill a large, medium, and small jar with the hot water. Let the jars set for an hour; then measure the temperature of the water in each jar with a thermometer or with your finger. Which jar has the warmest water and which one has the coldest? If these were three deer, which would still be warmest? Does this explain why deer might have evolved to be larger in the cold north than in the warmer south?

Look at the Deer, Dear

Does your Grandma or someone special sometimes call you "dear"? Do you notice anything different about how you, my *dear,* is spelled, and how the *deer* in the woods is spelled? Well, when two words are pronounced the same, but are spelled differently and mean different things, those words are called *homonyms.* Get a paper and pencil; write down as many homonyms as you can think of in five minutes. Then, at dinner ask your family if they can think of any more to add to your list. Here are a few to get you started: *here, hear; to, too, two; so, sew.* Now, you try it.

How Many Deer Are Too Many?

Every creature's habitat can only support a certain number of those creatures for any length of time. Biologists call this number the *carrying capacity* of the habitat. When there are more deer than the carrying capacity of their wintering areas, large numbers of deer will starve or be so weakened that they'll die of disease. But first they'll eat up every bit of browse, and it may take years to grow enough to support a normal number of deer again.

There's nothing natural about these sharp ups and downs in the deer population. Wolves and cougars, nature's deer *predators,* or hunters, kept the number of deer in balance with their habitat for thousands of years. But there are no wolves and cougars in large parts of North America today, because they don't mix well with people. Nowadays, human predators, or hunters, keep the deer in balance with their habitat, although some people are against deer hunting.

How long do you think most deer live? Life in the wild is very hard, and many fawns die during their first year, killed by predators, disease, or lack of food in severe winters. You may be surprised to know that the average life span of a deer is only about two years.

Be a Super Sleuth

Go into the woods when the leaves are off the trees in the early fall. Look for signs that deer may have been around. Study the tracks on page 76. Do you see any deer tracks in the soft soil? Look carefully at the low-growing shrubs and brush along the ground. Do you see any signs that deer may have been browsing? Look towards the treetops? Do you see open sky, or are there a lot of evergreen trees with thick branches overhead? From your observations, what conclusions can you make about whether deer have been in the woods and whether they might choose this as a deer wintering area?

THE MOOSE

FOOD KEY

BUDS & SOFT TWIGS

• RANGE MAP •

Not Too Close!

Nearly everyone enjoys seeing moose, the largest member of the deer family, because of their impressive size. Luckily, more and more people are getting a chance to see these great beasts since moose have returned in large numbers to northern New England and New York during the past few years.

Moose sometimes don't seem very frightened by people — especially in areas where moose have gotten used to seeing humans. Because of that, some people think moose are tame, so they walk right up to them — or even try to touch them. This is very dangerous! Moose are huge, powerful animals, and they are known to turn on people. They are also wild, and that means they're unpredictable.

The Moose Didn't Do It

When people see fewer deer around and more moose, they often think that the moose are driving out the deer. There's no evidence that this is true. What usually happens is that the deer's *habitat*, or preferred environment, has been changed for some reason — such as people cutting large areas of the forest. The new habitat (without large trees) favors moose instead of deer, so the deer either move on or die off, and the moose move in. For instance, if deer wintering areas have been logged, the deer may not be able to survive bad winters because they depend on the shelter the evergreen branches provide from the deep snow. But the much larger moose can plow through deep snow more easily, plus the young shoots coming up after logging make ideal moose food. Thus, because of the habitat change, there will be fewer deer and more moose. If people want to point a finger at who is responsible, they might just look in the mirror to find the culprit!

It's All ON My Head

Large bull moose have tremendous antlers. Use a tape measure to mark off four and a half feet. That's how wide a big set of moose antlers could be. And what about weight? Try to lift a fifty-pound bag of dog food or bird seed. Now imagine carrying that kind of size and weight around on your head. Moose are so big and strong that they can run through the woods with these great antlers and not even think about it!

Getting around: Have you ever tried to walk through a doorway with your arms full? Sometimes you have to turn sideways to fit through. Well, imagine how a moose has to move with his broad antlers on his head? See if you can find a yardstick or a three-to-four-foot stick around your house. Hold it on your head, so that half sticks out on each side. Now *very carefully* stand straight and tall, and walk slowly around. Be careful not to knock anything over or poke anyone near you. It's quite a challenge to maneuver around, isn't it? How do you suppose an enormous, majestic moose manages to run quickly and quietly through the forest carrying its wide load?

50 LBS

4 FEET

Pretty Is, as Pretty Does

Though people are impressed by the sheer size of a moose, people often refer to them as homely. That's because they look awkward, and because of the shape of their large, overhanging upper lip. Saying that a moose is homely misses the point, though; as you can see, the moose is wonderfully *adapted* (suited) to life in the harsh climate of the far north where it lives. In fact, if you think about it, the stately moose is a beautiful work of nature. Let's list the ways:

★

With their long, powerful legs, moose are wonderfully adapted to living in the deep snow.

★

When they browse, that big, overhanging upper lip becomes very useful. Moose just wrap it around a small branch and strip leaves, buds, the tip of the branch, and perhaps some of the bark off at a single pull. What could be more efficient for food gathering!

★

Moose are strong, fast swimmers. They often swim across ponds and lakes, rather than going around.

★

A moose's antlers are a form of *defense,* or protection, against predators or other bull moose. Notice how pointed, majestic, and wonderfully enormous they are!

★

Moose live a lot longer than deer. Some moose live into their teens and a very few may even live twenty years.

★

Habitat Happiness

Just as people like to live in certain places, animals have areas, or *habitats,* where they like to live, grow, and raise their young, too. But, too often, people clear the land or pollute the water, or change the natural character of a place without thinking about how it might affect the wildlife living there.

What do you think happens when people develop buildings, malls, and homes near the habitat of an animal like the moose? Will the water stay clean? Will the land support young shrubs for food?

Let's try to understand what happens when humans pollute the natural environment by seeing just how difficult it is to clean up water.

PLASTIC WRAP
SODA POP-TOPS

OLIVE OIL

DIRT
PEBBLES
TWIGS

FOOD
COLOR

STIRRER
STICK

5 GALLON BUCKET
FILLED WITH WATER

Fill a five-gallon bucket with water. Drop some dirt, twigs, plastic bag or wrap, soda pop-tops, olive oil, pebbles, and food coloring into the water. Stir with a stick. Then, using the tools listed below or other clever ideas you come up with, try to take the "pollution" out of the water.

Tools:

STRAINER

CHEESECLOTH

SPOON

SLOTTED SPOON

CLEAN
WATER

TONGS

Well, did you have any luck? Could you remove any of the pollution? Some of it? All of it? Which tools worked best? Was there a perfect tool that could completely do the job? When people pollute the water, even with our most modern water-cleaning methods and technologies, the water will never be as clean and fresh as it was before it was polluted.

That's the bad news, but the good news is that you and your friends and families can do a lot to improve the natural environment (you did get the water a little cleaner), and you can do a lot to make sure that more wildlife habitats are not polluted or damaged.

Palms Up

Moose antlers are very different from the antlers of most other members of the deer family because they're wide and flat, with points sticking out at the sides and ends. Open your hands wide, with the palms up. That's about how moose antlers look — in miniature, of course.

Finger paint fun: You can create a great set of antlers using your bare hands and colorful finger paints.

Here's what you'll need:

White paper, large enough to fit both hands side by side

Paper plate

Pencil, scrap newspaper, markers or crayons, finger paint

Cover the work area with newspaper. Fold the white paper in half vertically, make a crease down the middle, open the paper up, and place on newspaper. Cover the paper plate with a thin layer of finger paint. Place your right hand, palm down with fingers spread out in the paint, and then print on the white paper a little to the right of fold line, towards the top of the paper. Do the same thing with the other hand, and print on the upper left side. Press hard. These are the antlers for your moose picture. Now sketch in a moose face with a big nose and overhanging lips. Make it as realistic or as fanciful as you like. A moose is really a very dark brown — almost black — but color your moose with fun colors, if you wish.

FAMILY LIFE

The female moose (called a *cow*) usually mates with the dominant bull in her area and has one, two, or occasionally even three babies, called calves. The calves are very long-legged and weigh 25–35 pounds at birth. They gain weight very fast — as much as 2 pounds a day for the first 3 months — and weigh from 300 to 400 pounds by fall. Do you know a person who weighs about 200 pounds? How long did it take that person to become that large? A moose gets that big in less than five months!

The cow moose raises her calf or calves all by herself. Like other males in the deer family, the bull moose doesn't help at all with raising the calves. Moose winter in very small groups of two or three. A cow and her one or two calves may winter in one spot, and a bull or two in another.

Wanderlust

Moose sometimes show up in strange places, such as hanging out with a farmer's herd of cows, or wandering through the main streets of a town or city. That's especially true of young bulls in the fall. Biologists aren't sure why the young bulls wander so much, but it may be that they're trying to find a new territory where they can become the dominant bulls.

What's in a Name?

The word moose came from the Algonquin Indians of the Northeast. They called the animal *moosu,* which means "he trims or strips off" (leaves and bark). Isn't that a good description of the way moose feed? American Indians gave very clear, descriptive names to wildlife and to people. The names accurately described their observations, such as "Runs Like The Wind" for a long-legged, swift-moving child.

Name that animal: Here's something you can do when you and your family are riding in the car. Someone names an animal and everyone takes a turn giving it an American Indian-style name. When you get good at it, try it the other way around: first say the name, and have others guess what the animal is. Use your powers of observation.

HOW BIG IS BIG

How tall do you think a big bull moose is? Have an adult help you put a mark six and a half feet high on a tree or an outside wall. That's how tall a big bull's shoulders are. Then hold the bottom of a yardstick against that mark and look up to the top of the yardstick. That's how high the tips of a big bull's antlers can go — about nine and a half feet high! (If you are three feet tall, that means the bull moose is over three times taller.) A really big bull moose can also weigh 1,500 to 1,600 pounds. That's as much as the biggest brown and polar bears weigh. Another way of thinking about the size of a moose is that a full-grown deer, with its head lowered, can walk underneath the belly of a big moose. You're right if you think a moose is really huge!

6 ½

HOME SWEET HOME

Like deer, moose have a territory or home range — but moose are great travellers and roam over a much larger area than deer. Moose don't run in great leaps the way deer often do. Instead, they trot. Don't be fooled by their awkward appearance, either. They can trot at a steady clip; at top speed, they can go about 35 miles per hour for shorter distances. How fast is that? The next time you're riding in a car, ask the driver to travel at 35 miles an hour for a short distance. Notice how fast everything seems to pass you. Can you imagine running that fast?

Moose will live in many types of forest habitat, but they prefer areas with shallow ponds and boggy places (moose love underwater plants; in the summer, they'll stand in the water and put their entire heads underwater while they feed), plus lots of *browse,* or low-growing shrubs with bud tips to feed on.

THE MOOSE • 85

Wordly wise: Sometimes when we try to explain something to people, or when we write or tell a story, we use words like "big" or "small," but they don't really mean anything unless we give clearer information. We might say that a squirrel is bigger than a mouse, but we could also say that a moose is bigger than a mouse — a lot bigger! Next time you are describing something you saw to a friend, use comparisons so your friend will get a clear picture. Instead of saying, "I saw a really big squirrel at our bird feeder," you might say, "I saw a squirrel as big as my dog at our bird feeder." Now that was one big squirrel!

A Power Struggle

The males of all the members of the deer family, including moose, fight to become *dominant* (the boss or most powerful) during the *fall rut,* or mating season, when they protect their territory. Because of their great size and strength, a fight between two bull moose is an awesome sight. The angry bulls will thrash the brush with their great antlers, sometimes rooting up whole bushes and small trees, and tossing them in the air. Then, grunting ferociously, they'll charge each other, smash their antlers together, and shove each other around for minutes at a time to see which one is stronger.

THE BISON

Although everyone calls it a buffalo, this enormous beast is really a bison. The true buffalo are the *water buffalo* of Asia and the *Cape buffalo* of Africa. Can you find pictures of these in an encyclopedia or other book and compare them with the bison?

Many people believe that the American bison (we'll refer to it as a bison or a buffalo in this book) is an *endangered species,* or nearly extinct. The good news is that the American bison is doing very well and is increasing in numbers.

HOME SWEET HOME

Home, for buffalo, was mainly on the prairies — the great, grassy plains of what is now the central United States and Canada. However, buffalo also lived to the east and north of the prairies in partly wooded areas with occasional openings. Today, buffalo are raised here and there throughout all but the most northern parts of North America.

FAMILY LIFE

A buffalo cow has a single calf (twins are rare) in the spring. The calf gains strength very quickly and can keep up with its mother after only a few days. It makes sense that buffalo evolved in this way, because they're herd animals that travel a great deal and seldom linger long in one spot. If the calves couldn't keep pace with the herd at a very young age, the herd wouldn't be able to move fast enough to keep itself well fed.

The English language certainly can be confusing when it comes to speaking about more than one animal. When you form the plural (more than one) of many words, you simply add an "s," as when going from one *squirrel* to many *squirrels*. With the word bison, however, you talk about one *bison* or many *bison* — no "s" added! The same is true of *moose*. Now, how many other animals can you think of where the word stays the same when you are referring to one or many? How many can your whole family come up with? Some words have several different choices in forming the plural. The plural of buffalo can be spelled *buffalo, buffaloes,* or *buffalos* — and they are each correct! What about plurals formed by changing the whole word, as in one *mouse* and many *mice*? Ask a friend who speaks another language like Spanish, or French, or German, how they form plurals in their language.

One Bison, Two Bison

A WALK ON THE WILD SIDE

Would you like to see real, live buffalo? It's not that difficult, because there are people who raise buffalo in every state and province and are willing to have visitors come to see them. You can find out where to see buffalo by writing either the American Bison Association, P.O. Box 16660, Denver, Colorado 80216 or the National Buffalo Association, Box 580, Fort Pierre, South Dakota 57532. Both of these groups will also send you interesting information about buffalo. Charts showing all the things Indians used buffalo for are especially interesting.

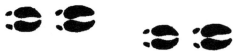

An Impressive Beast

Have you ever seen a picture of a buffalo? Most people have, and have also heard about the days when vast herds of these animals roamed the prairies. Have you ever noticed that in every picture of buffalo, they seem to hold their heads very low? That's because they can't raise their heads to the level of their shoulders.

A buffalo is an impressive beast, with its hump at the front shoulder, thick, shaggy fur on its head and front quarters, and its sharp, curving horns. Imagine what it must have been like to see a herd of these animals so huge that it took days to pass by! There are no longer enormous herds of buffalo roaming the plains, but there are plenty for us to see and to insure that the species will survive.

Have you ever seen a cow swish flies off itself with its long tail? Well, buffalos have short tails that aren't very effective in keeping off flies, so they make *wallows* — places where they can roll in the dust or mud to get rid of biting insects.

Bison Sculpture

Make a bison out of modeling clay. Pay particular attention to the shape of its head, front quarters, and its horns. Make its fur with a toothpick. Should its head be higher than its shoulders?

●

NATIVE AMERICAN LEGENDS

Buffalo were of the greatest importance to the Plains Indians, so it's no surprise that they told many stories about them. Here's one from the Cheyenne of what is now Wyoming, Nebraska, and the Dakotas (see page 146 for another).

●

After the world was created, buffalo became too proud and began to think they were the most powerful creatures in the world. They began to eat other animals, even humans. The people thought this was unfair and complained, so the buffalo proposed a race to see who was faster, buffalo or people.

Because humans have only two legs, the four-legged buffalo allowed the people to have birds race in their place. The race was a very close one, but in the end a magpie finished just ahead of the fastest buffalo. Since that race, people have been more powerful than buffalo and have hunted buffalo for food.

●

A good example: This is a wonderful legend because it shows how the American Indians used storytelling to try to explain something very difficult to understand — how humans were able to kill animals as huge as buffalo for their food. Now, you create a legend that explains something you find very difficult to understand. It can be about wildlife or it can be about anything in your life that puzzles you. Write your legend down or record it onto a tape.

Make A Difference!

The biggest problem for wild bison is finding enough grazing land. The Wild Bison Foundation is trying to buy grazing rights from ranchers in Utah's Henry Mountains so that the bison can use the land. For $25 you can be part of their Adopt-A-Bison program. For more information, contact the Wild Bison Foundation, P.O. Box 27846, Salt Lake City, Utah 84127.

Cash for causes: The Adopt-A-Bison program is just one of many good causes that you might be interested in for wildlife preservation, conservation, and the good of the earth. If you want to get involved, there are all sorts of things you can do to raise a little spare money to contribute to these organizations. First though, ask a grown-up to help you check that the organization uses contributions properly, and be sure it is all right with the grown-up at your house if you do this. Then, get organized. Ask a friend or your brother or sister to become involved. Perhaps, you could clean up your neighborhood and return empty bottles for the deposit. Or, maybe you can feed a neighbor's cat, water their plants, or walk their dog. Or, put up a sign offering to weed gardens or rake leaves. You will be helping not only an organization but someone in your neighborhood, too. Whatever you do, do a good job so you will be asked back again.

Fenced In, But Not Tame

Like so many other wild animals that become used to seeing humans, buffalo often act quite tame — but don't let that fool you! Every year people are seriously injured at places like Yellowstone National Park when they try to get too close to buffalo. Just because buffalo frequently live in fenced-in places now, doesn't mean that they are tame. They are still very, very dangerous, so never try to get close to one, no matter how friendly it appears.

You can often predict a buffalo's actions by its tail. The more excited, alarmed, or angry a buffalo becomes, the higher it lifts its tail. When its tail points almost straight up, it's apt to be very dangerous!

Make a Plains Indian Diorama

Imagine that you're a Plains Indian — one of the many tribes inhabiting the prairies — living while there were still great herds of buffalo. What sort of home would you have? What would your clothes be made of? What would you eat, and what would you use for tools and weapons? How many of these things would you get from the buffalo, and how important would the buffalo be in your life? What weapons would you use to kill buffalo for the things you needed in order to live?

Make a shoe box diorama showing as much as you can about the buffalo and life on the prairies. Stand a shoe box on its side, in its lid. Paint the outside any color you wish or wrap in old gift wrap. Inside, paint a background and sky, plus a foreground. Then, using twigs, dried grasses, pebbles, clay, toothpicks, scraps of cloth and yarn, and plenty of your own imagination, create a Plains Indian scene with lots of buffalo. Put your diorama on a bookcase for all to enjoy.

Environmentally Yours

Estimates of the number of bison in North America before the coming of the European settlers range from 30 million to 200 million animals! Sixty million is the most common estimate, though. Buffalo numbers didn't change much until the American Civil War ended in 1865. Then railroads were built across the continent, and buffalo were shot by the millions to feed railroad workers and to make warm buffalo robes. There were no game laws in those days, and the buffalo were simply killed off without any thought for the future.

Incredible as it seems, there were so few buffalo left after just a few short years that it appeared they would become extinct. Luckily, a few early conservationists and conservation-minded ranchers protected the few remaining buffalo — probably only about one hundred wild ones and a few hundred more on private ranches.

Today there are about 150,000 bison in North America, and at least a few can be found in every state and province, including Alaska. About 17,000 of these are in parks, refuges, and other public land; the rest are on private ranches. There are three herds that are still wild and completely unfenced. One is in Yellowstone National Park, one in the Henry Mountains Wilderness of southern Utah, and the third in the Kaibab National Forest of Arizona. There is also a wild herd of *Wood Buffalo* (a very closely related species) in Canada's Wood Buffalo Park — the same park where whooping cranes spend the summer. Wood buffalo are longer than the American buffalo and have higher, heavier hind quarters. Otherwise, they look much like the American buffalo.

FUN FACTS

The United States once had a nickel with a buffalo on it. It was made from 1935 to 1938. There are still a few around; perhaps you've seen one, or can find one in someone's coin collection.

★

All adult buffalo are big, but the older bulls are especially large. A really huge bull can stand over six feet high at the front shoulder and weigh more than 2,000 pounds. That makes the buffalo the largest land mammal in North America — even larger than the largest moose, brown bear, or polar bear!

Most wild animals, even large ones, don't live very long, but bison are an exception. Buffalo cows usually live twenty to twenty-five years, and a few live for more than thirty years. The bulls usually have a shorter life span.

HOW BIG IS BIG

UNITED STATES OF AMERICA

FIVE CENTS

THE THREE BEARS

Don't Feed or Pet the Bears – Ever!

No, this isn't a fairy tale about a little girl named Goldilocks and the three bears whose house she found in the woods. Instead, it's about three *species* (kinds) of real bears that live in North America. They are the black bear, the brown bear — which includes the grizzly and the coastal brownie — and the polar bear.

If you go to a national park, state park, or public campground, you may see bears hanging around and begging for food. If you do, DON'T TRY TO FEED OR PET THEM. These are not tame bears, even though they've lost their natural fear of humans. Every year a number of people are injured, some of them seriously, by these "tame" bears. Enjoy watching them, but don't ever try to go near them.

Bears don't attack very often, though, if they are left alone. Most black bears would rather run away than attack a human. However, mothers with cubs sometimes attack because they want to protect the cubs. Grizzly bears are much more apt to attack humans than are other kinds of bears and should be considered extremely dangerous. But all bears are big, strong animals that can be dangerous, so keep your distance from them.

Only black bears can climb trees. Other bears stay on the ground, and people have escaped attacking grizzly bears, for example, by climbing the nearest tree. No one is sure how the story got started that bears can't run fast downhill, but it definitely isn't true. Bears can run very fast — much faster than any human — either uphill or down!

NATIVE AMERICAN LEGENDS

The Loucheux tell this wonderful legend about how the bear got such a short, stubby tail.

●

The bear once had a long, furry tail. Then he asked the fox how to catch crayfish. The tricky fox told the bear to hang his long tail in the water through a hole in the ice until the crayfish pinched it. Then he could pull them up on his tail.

The bear did as the fox told him, but when he felt a pinch on his tail, it was the ice freezing around it. When he finally tried to pull his tail out, it was frozen hard into the ice! The bear yanked hard and broke his tail off near the base — and has had a short tail ever since.

●

Fact or fiction: As you can see, this Native American legend is based on true observations of bears (bears do have stubbed tails). Legends use close observations of nature to attempt to explain in a story what otherwise would be unexplainable. Writing your own legends is a very good way to use the information you learn in this book and from your own observations during walks.

There are also a lot of stories about bears that aren't based on facts; instead they are based on the author's feelings and imagination. For example, *Father Bear Comes Home* by Else Holmelund Minarik isn't based on truth — father bears don't even live with their cubs — but it is a wonderful story about a child-bear and her father just the same. These stories, called *fiction* (which means they are made up and aren't true), can be a lot of fun to listen to, read, write, or act out. Make a list of all the bear stories you can think of. Can you think of as many as three? five? ten? Go to the library and read or listen to your favorite bear story and also one brand new one that you've never heard before.

— FACT —

— FICTION —

Alike and Different

Although black bears, brown bears, and polar bears are different in many ways, they also have a lot in common. When we talk about what is alike, we are talking about how they are *similar,* or their *similarities.* The ways that they are unlike, or different, are their *differences.*

★

BLACK BEAR

Meet the Bears

Many misunderstandings have grown up about bears. For instance, many people think that bears eat mostly meat. Except for the polar bear, the opposite is usually true. Bears certainly enjoy meat if they can get it, but they mostly eat many kinds of plant materials, such as nuts, berries, wetland (or marsh) plants, and grasses. The bears of North America are considered *predators* because they kill and eat other creatures, which are called their *prey*.

★

• RANGE MAP •

FOOD KEY

- GREEN PLANTS
- BERRIES
- BEECH-NUTS + ACORNS
- ANTS
- MICE
- FAWN

Black bear: The *black bear* is by far our most common bear. Black bears live in many kinds of habitat and can sometimes be found surprisingly close to large cities. Except around parks and other places where bears become used to a lot of people, black bears are usually very shy. They will run at the first sign of a human, and many people who have spent years in the woods have never seen a black bear. It's impossible to count all the black bears in North America, but biologists estimate there are 500,000 – 750,000 black bears!

POLAR BEAR

Polar bear: These are the most unusual of all the bears because they live in the most unusual place — the cold, snowy Arctic not far from the North Pole. When you think of what this area is like, with vast expanses of snow, ice, and ocean, and very few plants, is it any wonder that polar bears are so different from other bears?

Polar bears are wonderful swimmers and have been seen miles from any land or solid ice. Most of their swimming is done with their huge front paws, which make great paddles. Polar bears have a thick mat of underhair that traps air and holds the bear high in the water, something like the way a life jacket holds you up. This thick fur also keeps the icy water away from the bear's skin.

A polar bear will wait for hours by a breathing hole in the ice to catch a seal — its main food — when it comes up for air. To stalk a seal on the ice, a polar bear will flatten its head and body against the ice, tucking its front paws underneath, and push itself along with its hind feet. Imagine what a sight that is!

FOOD KEY

SEALS

BIRDS' EGGS

BERRIES

• RANGE MAP •

• RANGE MAP •

■ Grizzly Bear □ Coastal Brown Bear

BROWN BEARS

FOOD KEY

🌿 GREEN PLANTS

🦌 FAWN

🐀 RODENTS

🐞 LADY BUG BEETLES

🦋 MOTH LARVAE

Brown bear: The *brown bears* are divided into two smaller groups — the *grizzly* and the *coastal brown bear*. Although most biologists think they are part of one species, these two groups have quite a few differences. Grizzlies live inland, away from the ocean. This is very different from the habitat of the coastal brown bears and that probably accounts for many of their differences. Grizzlies have whitish tips on their hair, especially on the back, and this gives them a *grizzled* look (grizzled means streaked with gray). Grizzlies eat more meat than black bears, although plants still make up most of their diet.

The coastal brown bears, as the name suggests, live close to the ocean. That probably has a lot to do with such things as their size and what they eat. Coastal brownies look much browner than grizzlies. They eat a lot more meat than either black bears or the inland grizzlies. They feed on things like stranded whales and dead seals, and they especially love to catch spawning salmon, a very rich food, which may be the reason the coastal brownie grows so much bigger than the grizzly.

GRIZZLY BEAR

FOOD KEY

- DEAD WHALES
- SALMON
- GREEN PLANTS

Check My Coat

Some bears aren't quite what they seem. Did you know that not all black bears are black? They're sometimes brown, especially in the West, and are often called *cinnamon bears.* These are still the same species as the black bear, however, so don't confuse them with the much larger, true brown bear.

Did you know that polar bears aren't really white? Not many people do. The polar bear's long outer hairs aren't actually colored white, but they look it because the center of each outer hair carries light that filters out through the sides and makes the hair appear white. This system carries sunlight right down to the polar bear's black skin, where it can absorb the sun's heat.

The polar bear has evolved with this wonderful *adaptation,* which gives it the best of two worlds. An adaptation is a special quality that gives a creature a better chance to survive. If the bear were really white, it would reflect the sun's rays and heat, and it might freeze in the terrible Arctic cold. If it looked dark-colored, it wouldn't be able to sneak up on seals to catch them. But with this amazing adaptation, the polar bear can stay warm and catch its prey at the same time.

Polar bear science: Take two jars the same size and fill one with milk, the other with strong coffee or some other dark-colored liquid. Set them aside until they both are at room temperature. Now put both jars in the sun for an hour or two. Then measure the temperature of each with a food thermometer. Which is warmer? Why?

Next, fill both jars with the dark liquid. Cover one with a white cloth and the other with something transparent, such as plastic wrap. Put them both in the sun for an hour or two and measure the temperature of each. Which is warmer, and why? How do these two experiments help to explain how polar bears, with their wonderful fur, can survive in the bitter Arctic cold?

★

COASTAL BROWN BEAR

HOW HUGE IS HUGE?

It's hard to believe that those tiny bear cubs that only weigh a few ounces can grow to be so huge, but they certainly can. Black bears are the smallest of the three North American species, with adults usually weighing from 150 to 400 pounds. Grizzly bears are much larger than black bears, weighing from 300 to 900 pounds or more.

Huge is the right word for the monster coastal brown bears and polar bears, which can weigh as much as 1,500 pounds. That's about as much as eight

COASTAL BROWN BEAR   POLAR BEAR   GRIZZLY BEAR   BLACK BEAR

full-grown men put together would weigh! When a big coastal brownie stands straight up on its hind legs, its head may be nearly as high as a regulation basketball hoop — ten feet off the floor! Some biologists think the coastal brownie is the largest bear in the world, although others believe polar bears may grow as large.

Make a bear graph: When you are given measurable information about several different things — such as the weight of four different bears — a *bar graph* can help you see, or visualize, what these numbers mean. Let's do a bar graph comparing adult bear weights. You'll need a ruler and a piece of paper, plus some crayons or markers if you want to color in your bars. Let ½" equal 250 pounds on your graph.

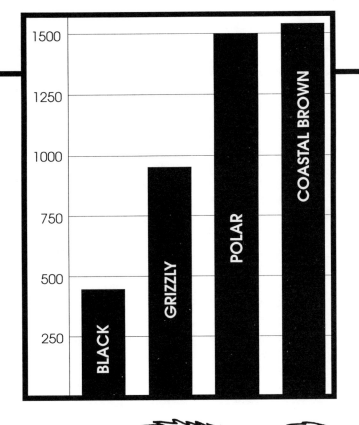

Although most North American bears seem to be holding their own, the grizzly bears in the lower forty-eight states are threatened. There are only about a thousand of these magnificent animals left in and around Glacier and Yellowstone National Parks.

The main threat comes from development — hotels, tourist lodges, restaurants, and other things to attract, house, and feed people. Each new development nibbles away at the habitat the grizzlies need in order to live. We will have to choose whether to have bears or more and more development around these two parks.

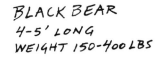

BLACK BEAR
4-5' LONG
WEIGHT 150-400 LBS

GRIZZLY BEAR
6-7½' LONG
WEIGHT 300-900 LBS

POLAR BEAR
6-8' LONG
WEIGHT UP TO 1500 LBS

COASTAL BROWN BEAR
6-8½' LONG
WEIGHT UP TO 1600 LBS

★ Favorite ★ Pretend Bears

Do you have a favorite Teddy bear? Lots of people of all ages do. Did you ever wonder where the name Teddy bear came from? Well, the twenty-sixth president of the United States was named Theodore (Teddy for short) Roosevelt. In 1902, he went bear hunting, but he couldn't catch a bear, except for a bedraggled-looking bear that some dogs had chased. He refused to kill the bear under such unsporting conditions. A newspaper ran a cartoon about this hunting incident. That inspired Morris Michtom, who ran a toy shop in Brooklyn, NY, to create a cuddly stuffed bear. Supposedly, Mr. Michtom wrote the president to use his name for his stuffed bears. President Roosevelt is said to have replied, "I don't think my name will mean much to the bear business, but you're welcome to use it." And they've been called Teddy bears ever since!

HOME SWEET HOME

During the warm months, bears don't really have a home. Instead, they have a *territory*, a large area, often many miles across, where they travel for food.

It's a different story in cold weather, though. Then most bears, except those in very warm places like Florida, seek a den in which to spend the winter, and males and females den separately. Often a den is nothing more than a little shelter under the roots of a fallen tree, or a hollow in the ground. Bears will use a cave for a den if they can find one, but caves are scarce in most places, so most bears don't den in caves and they often rely on their thick fur and a layer of fat to keep them from freezing.

In areas where there are summer cottages closed up for the winter, black bears some-times den under porches! In places where the cold isn't extreme, they also build huge nests on the ground. These are made of leaves and grass, and the bear simply curls up in it for the winter.

Grizzly bears den later than black bears and come out earlier. Usually they den at high altitude — 6,000 to 7,000 feet — by digging into a steep slope. Coastal brown bears den much like grizzlies, except not so high up in the mountains.

Unlike other bears, only the pregnant female polar bears den. The pregnant females often dig out a den in a big snowbank or in a bed of peat. However, they sometimes just lie on the snow and let falling and drifting snow cover them.

A WALK ON THE WILD SIDE

Walk in the woods and see how many places you can find where a bear might den. Look for things like uprooted trees, caves, deep hollows in the ground, or a fox or coyote den which a bear might dig out to make it bigger. Imagine that you are a bear. Which of the places you've found do you think would make the best winter den?

FAMILY LIFE

Male bears live alone almost all year. Only in the summer do they come together with the females for a short time to mate. Then they go their solitary way again, and take no part in raising the cubs. Indeed, male bears will even kill a cub if they get the chance, and female bears will fight the males fiercely to keep them away from their cubs.

Bears have a very unusual trait. Although they mate in the summer, the fertile eggs don't begin to grow inside the mother until late fall. Then, if the mother doesn't get enough good food in the fall, the cubs won't develop inside her. This helps female bears to survive in years when food is scarce, because they wouldn't have enough fat stored to nourish themselves and their cubs through the long winter.

BEAR ALERT
STOP DON'T WALK IN THIS AREA

Hibernation: A Light Sleep

The cubs are born in the den during hibernation. Because of this, many people have the idea the mother bear is so sound asleep that she doesn't even know when her cubs are born. This isn't true. Bears are not like woodchucks, which go into a very deep sleep during hibernation. Instead, they wake up often and occasionally even leave their dens for a short while. At any rate, the mothers certainly know when their cubs are born and take good care of their babies in the den.

Hibernation heartbeat: When a bear hibernates in the winter, its pulse or heartbeat slows down to help the bear save energy. Your pulse doesn't slow down this much when you sleep, but it is slower than when you are active. Find out how low your pulse is when you wake up in the morning by gently pressing your thumb to the side of your neck in the groove beneath your jawbone. You'll feel your heart beating a pulse or surge of blood through your artery. For 60 seconds, count how many times your heart beats. Then at another time during the day, when you're more active, stop to take your pulse again. Is it higher? A hibernating bear's heart beats about eight times per minute when the bear is sound asleep. How does that compare with your resting heart rate?

Tiny Bear Cubs

Do you know about how big a human baby is when it's born? Full-grown bears are so much bigger than humans that you might expect their newborn cubs to be much bigger than human babies — but bear cubs are tiny. You could probably hold two newborn black bear cubs in your hands! Cubs of brown and polar bears are a little bigger, but you could still hold one in your hands quite easily. Like kittens, bear cubs don't open their eyes for a few days after they're born.

Bears don't have cubs every year. Black bears usually have two cubs every other year; they stay with their mother for a year and a half. Brown bears have two or three cubs, but only every three years. They stay with their mother for two and a half years. Polar bears usually have two cubs every two or three years.

Would you like to live in a snow house? Lots of polar bear cubs spend the first months of their lives protected from the terrible Arctic cold and storms in a snow den, cozy beside their mother.

THE GRAY OR TIMBER WOLF

• RANGE MAP •

FOOD KEY

SMALL ANIMALS

LARGE ANIMALS

There is something special about wolves that seems to make many people either love them or hate them. Perhaps it's because so few people really understand what wolves are like. The fact is that wolves are neither good nor bad — they're just wild animals. They *prey* on,

or kill, other animals in order to eat and survive, not because wolves are cruel. Usually wolves kill old, weak, or sick animals because those are the easiest to catch — and they kill the very young for the same reason. But they'll also go after healthy wild animals, as well as cattle, sheep, and pets, when they get the chance. The wolves don't know the difference — to them, a cow just seems like a slow deer or moose! In fact, wolves can't live without hunting big prey. And, in spite of fairy tales like *Little Red Riding Hood,* truly wild wolves almost never attack humans. However, so-called "tame" captive wolves and wolf-dog crosses have killed or badly injured a number of children. You should consider them very dangerous and stay well out of their reach.

Who's Top Wolf around Here?

Have you read about places where a king and queen rule the country, with dukes and duchesses below them, and the peasants at the bottom? Well, a wolf pack is run in much the same way. The "king and queen" wolves are called the *alpha* male and female. They're usually the oldest wolves in the pack. They boss the others and decide when and where the pack should hunt and which animals to attack. The alpha wolves may also decide to call off an attack when they think it will be unsuccessful because the prey is too strong and healthy.

Usually only the alpha male and female in a pack mate and have pups. The alpha male and female also get the most and the best meat after a kill.

Each wolf below the alpha pair tries to boss the wolves below itself. The unlucky wolf at the bottom is called an *omega* wolf and is pushed around by all the other wolves. Sometimes it's picked on so much that it leaves the pack and becomes an outcast lone wolf. Do you sometimes feel like the powerful alpha wolf, and sometimes feel like the picked-on omega wolf? Everyone has some days like that.

There's a good reason why biologists chose the names *alpha* and *omega* for the top and bottom wolves in a pack. Alpha is the first letter of the Greek alphabet, and the alpha wolves are first in the pack (our word *alphabet* comes from *alpha* and *beta*, the first two Greek letters). *Omega* is the last letter in the Greek alphabet, and of course the omega wolf is last in the pack's social order.

Although wolves sleep outdoors, the alpha female wolf moves into a den like a cave or burrow to raise her pups. There are usually five or six pups in a litter, each weighing only about a pound. They are both blind and deaf at birth, but they can see after two weeks, and they can hear about a week later. Their baby teeth break through at the same time, and they begin to eat small pieces of meat.

The life of the pack centers on the pups; the alpha male and other members of the pack bring food for the growing pups. It's a little like many human families, where brothers, sisters, aunts, uncles, and cousins baby-sit and do other things to help parents raise their children.

When the pups are about two months old, already weighing 15 – 20 pounds, they are moved to a *rendezvous* (RAHN-day-voo) site — a sheltered spot out of the den. (*Rendezvous* is a French word meaning a meeting place.) The pups stay at one or more rendezvous sites until early fall, when they begin to travel and hunt more and more with the pack. By the time they are a year old, they're nearly full grown.

ALPHA

OMEGA

Create a Track Story

Wolves are one of the few predators big, strong, and smart enough to prey on very large animals like deer, moose, elk, caribou, and bison (buffalo). It takes an unusual predator to be able to attack and kill such large animals, and that's one of the reasons why the wolf is so interesting.

It's dangerous for wolves to attack large prey. Wolves first stalk large prey to see if it will run. If it does, they will pursue it — sometimes for hours if they sense it is weakening. They'll also try to bite its hindquarters to slow it down. When the prey finally stops, a wolf — usually the alpha male — grabs it by the nose. Then the other pack members close in and bite it until it's finally brought down and killed.

Create a story by drawing wolf tracks and tracks of other animals that they prey on. Use the examples of real tracks found on the border of each page to help you draw authentic animal tracks for your story. Use symbols to represent a stream, a trampled area of grass or snow, kinds of trees and shrubs, a fight for survival, or whatever it is you want your tracks and symbols to tell.

When you're finished, have your friends "read" what the story is about and what happened based on the kinds of symbols and tracks you used. What kinds of animals would be in your wolf story? Where would they live? What time of year is it?

How long do you think a large, full-grown wolf is, and how much do you think it weighs? Most people think wild animals are much larger than they really are, and wolves are no exception.

A very large male wolf in Canada or Alaska is about 5½ feet long from the tip of its nose to the tip of its tail, and may weigh as much as 135 pounds. Females are a little smaller. Wolves that live farther south may weigh only 60 pounds or so — and in the Middle East as little as 30 pounds! Do you think this difference in weight between northern and southern wolves has anything to do with keeping warm in winter?

Do the experiment on page 76. Do you think northern wolves and northern deer have adapted to their climates in the same way?

Join the Pack

Most wolves live in groups called *packs* of about eight or ten wolves, but wolf packs in the far north sometimes have twenty or more wolves. A wolf pack is really a big family, with almost all the wolves in it related to each other — almost like parents, children, aunts and uncles, and cousins. They stick together and help each other, much as human families do.

Each wolf pack lives and hunts in its own territory. The size of this territory — anywhere from 5 to 30 square miles — depends on how abundant big game animals are. A wolf pack defends its territory against other wolves by fighting any other pack that tries to move in. These territorial fights can be so fierce that wolves sometimes kill each other (see also *Let's Talk About It*).

Putting It Together

Although the wolf is called the *gray wolf*, it's by no means always that color. Gray is the most common, but there are also many wolves that are either black or white. Here's a way to draw a gray wolf, and then remember its features for a long time to come.

Here's what you'll need:

Lightweight cardboard
(cereal boxes work well)

Plain paper, 8 1/2" x 11", any color

Markers, glue or paste, scissors

Using the illustration as an example, draw a wolf in its habitat on the paper. Look carefully at its shape and features, so that you'll always remember what a wolf looks like. Now, glue the paper to the blank side of the cardboard and trim both to the same size. On the opposite side, draw a puzzle pattern with a marker. Be sure the "pieces" are big enough to cut easily. When glue is dry, cut out the pieces, mix them all up, and then assemble your puzzle.

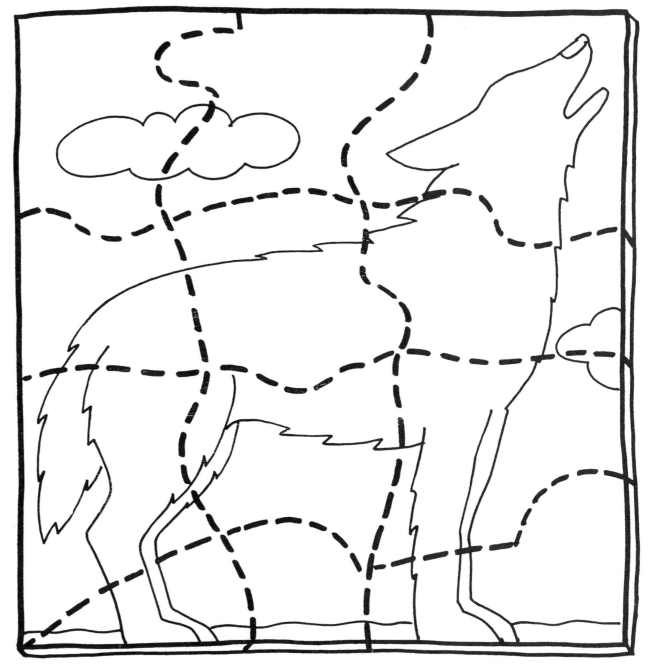

Pack Your Bags

Would you like to learn more about wolves and perhaps hear or even see one? Then visit the International Wolf Center in Ely, Minnesota. This center is a wonderful place to learn about wolves. It has wolf exhibits and video shows, and, even more exciting, it offers hikes to find signs of wolves, evening trips to hear wolves howl, and winter ski, snowshoe, or even dogsled trips into wolf country!

If you live close to an area where there are wolves, get in touch with your state or provincial wildlife agency, or a conservation organization. Ask them where you can go to hear wolves howl, see wolf tracks, or perhaps even catch sight of a wolf.

Learning more: There are two excellent videos about wolves that you can enjoy. One is *Following the Tundra Wolf;* the other is a National Geographic Explorer Video called *White Wolf.* Unlike some popular movies and videos, these two give accurate and fascinating information about wolves.

The Ancestral Trail

People often say that wolves are a member of the dog family, but that's really putting things backward. Actually, wolves came first and are the ancestors of our domestic dogs. No one knows exactly when, but a few thousand years ago people managed to tame some wolves, perhaps to help kill game for food and clothing. That means all of our domestic dogs, whether the tiny Chihuahua or the huge St. Bernard, descended from wolves that were tamed. Go to the library and ask for a book with pictures of dog breeds. Do you think there are any breeds of dogs that look a lot like wolves? Make a list of them and then draw them. Then, compare them carefully with the wolf. What looks the same? What looks different?

LET'S TALK ABOUT IT

In order for the pack to live, hunt, feed, and raise pups together, they need to "talk" to each other. Of course, they don't talk the way we do, using words. Instead, they use a variety of sounds, body movements, facial expressions, and scent to communicate.

When we think of wolves, we think of howling, and howling is certainly an important way in which wolves communicate. Howling helps wolves locate each other when they're scattered. Wolves may howl in a chorus when the pack is together, too. This howling warns other wolves to stay out of the pack's territory — but sometimes wolves just seem to howl in chorus because they enjoy it as a social activity.

Wolves often point their noses in the air when they howl, but it has nothing to do with the moon, even on a moonlit night. Probably that story started with people who watched wolves howl on a night when there was a full moon — and thought the moon was the reason for the howling.

Wolves use body movements and facial expressions, too. Usually the alpha wolves hold their tails straight out, while other wolves let their tails droop. When your dog is happy, it probably opens its mouth and lets its tongue hang out, and wolves do exactly the same thing. Wolves also show their teeth, growl, snarl, and raise the hair on their shoulders when they're angry, just as most dogs do.

Wolves also communicate by scent. For instance, they often urinate around the edges of their territory. This warns other wolves that the territory is taken, so stay away — or else! Do you

have a male dog? If so, you've probably seen him urinate on different objects by raising a hind leg. Your dog is showing his wolf ancestry and marking HIS territory.

Non-speak: How well do you think you can communicate without using words? Pick a time to take the non-speak test. (It's fun if you do this with your family or some friends.) Tell a grown-up what you are doing, and that you won't be speaking any words for an hour. Now, how will you communicate? Use your hands, your face, your whole body to let people know what you are thinking, what you need help with, what you are feeling, but don't speak (unless it's an emergency, of course).

Sponsor a Wolf

People become very angry when wolves kill their cattle, sheep, and pets. That's why wolves and people just don't mix around homes, farms, and ranches. The only place where wolves and people can get along is in large wilderness areas, where wolves and other truly wild animals, such as grizzly bears, can survive. If we lose our wilderness areas, we'll lose the wolves, too.

When an animal population diminishes, as has happened with the gray wolf in some areas, it becomes an *endangered species,* which means that there are still wolves around, but in some areas they could become extinct. If an animal becomes *completely extinct,* it means that there are no more of the animal left anywhere on earth.

Wolves are listed as an endangered species in the lower forty-eight states of the United States, except for Minnesota. However, there are still a lot of wolves in parts of North America, such as Canada (50,000), Alaska (7,000), and Minnesota (1500).

The U. S. Fish and Wildlife Service wants to restore wolves to northwestern Montana, central Idaho, and Yellowstone National Park — all places where there is a large wilderness area. Their goal is to have from 100 to 150 wolves in each of these three areas.

You can join a program created to help protect wolves in captive packs. Write to any of these organizations for more information, or if you'd like to help.

Wolf Sanctuary
Wild Canid Survival and Residence Center
P.O. Box 760
Eureka, MO 63025

National Wildlife Federation
1400 16th St. NW
Washington, D.C. 20036-2266

Wolf Haven
311 Offut Lake Rd.
Tenino, WA 98589

DOG?   WOLF?

THE BOBCAT AND THE LYNX

RANGE MAP

- Bobcat
- Lynx
- Both Bobcat and Lynx

FOOD KEY

- SNOW-SHOE HARE
- DEER
- MICE

LYNX

Do you know what a *first cousin* is? It's a very close relative — the daughters and sons of your aunts and uncles. The bobcat and lynx are about that closely related to each other. Sometimes first cousins have the same last names. That's also true of these two cats; the full name of the lynx is *Canada lynx,* and the full name of the bobcat is *bay lynx.*

The Canada lynx got its name because it lives mostly in Canada, but how did the bobcat get the name *bay lynx*? It's because bay is a reddish-brown color, and the bobcat's coat is often a light bay. The Canada lynx isn't brown, like the bobcat, but has a coat that's gray.

LYNX TRACKS

BOBCAT TRACKS

LYNX

BOBCAT

Deceiving Appearances

The bobcat and lynx are different in many ways, even though they're such close relatives. The lynx may *look* a lot bigger and fiercer than the bobcat because of its thick fur, long legs, huge feet, long ear tufts, and big ruff of fur around its face, but the truth is very different.

Bobcats weigh 15 – 35 pounds, which is actually a little more than lynx at 15 – 30 pounds, and they're a more powerful animal — capable of killing deer. A big male bobcat may reach fifty pounds or more, although that's unusual. The lynx is a few inches longer and taller than the bobcat, and, counting the thick fur at the edges, its great feet are more than four inches wide — twice the size of the bobcat's. Yet, whenever these two cat cousins meet, it's usually the lynx that backs down from the more aggressive bobcat.

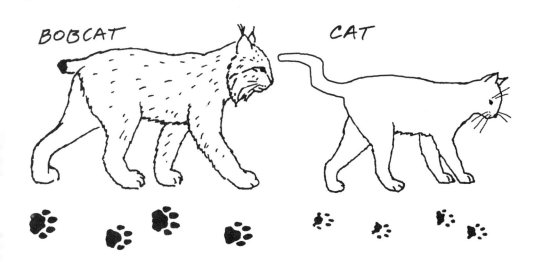

BOBCAT

CAT

Drawing to scale: Look at the paw or a footprint of a domestic cat. The shape of bobcat and lynx paws (see tracks on page border) is the same as that for domestic cats, only bigger. To draw them *to scale* which means to draw them in a way that shows the relationship of size, use a ruler to measure four inches. That's how big your lynx track should be. Now measure two inches. That's about how big your bobcat track should be. How big do you think your cat tracks should be? Which of these cats can get along better in soft, deep snow? Why? (For more on size relationships and scale, see page 29.)

NATIVE AMERICAN LEGENDS

Snowshoe Walk

In the wintertime, the lynx is able to walk easily on top of the snow. Its large paws distribute the weight of the cat over a larger area so it doesn't fall through the top surface. This is especially helpful when running after prey.

Make a pair of cardboard snowshoes and try walking atop some snow or sand. Get two shoe boxes or pieces of cardboard. Punch 2 holes in each shoe box or piece of cardboard, loop the string through each hole, and fasten. Wrap the string around the top of each shoe and tie it. Now try walking on the snow or in the sand. Do you tend to sink less than if you only had on street shoes?

The Algonquins of northeastern North America tell a wonderful story about the wildcat (bobcat or lynx).

The wildcat went hunting for Mahtigwess, the Great Rabbit, who was a mighty trickster. Over and over Mahtigwess fooled the cat with various disguises, such as appearing as an Indian chief. Finally the cat became so angry that he swore by his tail to catch and eat the Great Rabbit. But Mahtigwess continued to trick the cat, and because the cat had sworn by his tail to catch Mahtigwess, his tail fell off — and that's why the wildcat has such a short, stubby tail.

The Shawnees of the Ohio River Valley also had a legend about the bobcat.

The bobcat trapped a rabbit in a hollow log and said he would wait until the rabbit came out for food — then catch and eat him. The clever rabbit told the bobcat to build a fire so he could roast the rabbit. When the fire had lots of coals, the rabbit sprang into the fire and right back out, scattering hot coals all over the bobcat. The bobcat jumped into the river to quench the burning coals, but a spot was left on his coat wherever a hot coal had landed — and that's why bobcats have spotted coats!

■

Memory helpers: Do you ever make up rhymes or secret codes to help remember something more clearly? For example, you might remember that the bobcat mainly lives in the United States (the lynx is mainly in Canada), by remembering *B*obcat *U*nited *S*tates, or *BUS*. These are called *mnemonic devices* (ni-MAH-nik), or memory helpers. Notice how the story of how the bobcat got his spots is a mnemonic device — it is easy to remember now that bobcats are spotted. How might you remember that a lynx is *longer* than a bobcat: *l*ong *l*ynx — the two "L's" will make the connection for you. See how many memory helpers you can come up with that will make the wildlife in this book unforgettable? Use rhymes, stories, riddles, things that are familiar to you — anything goes if it jogs your memory.

Ancient Ancestors

Like the weasel family, fossils of the cat family date back forty million (40,000,000) years. There's a difference, though; the ancient ancestors of most mammals didn't look much like their modern descendants, but the cat ancestors looked enough like modern cats so that we'd recognize them as cats even today.

A 3-D cat mobile: The bobcat and lynx are just two relatives of the large cat family. Of course, you may have one member living in your home — that is if you have a domestic cat. Do you know who some of the others are? If you named the lion, tiger, leopard, jaguar, cougar and cheetah, you were exactly right. To make a cat mobile, first look in a book or encyclopedia for pictures of each of these wonderful creatures.

Here's what you'll need:

A stick or twig about 18 inches long
Paper — any size and colors
Cotton balls
Pencil, markers, glue, scissors
Yarn or string

Fold some pieces of paper in half, draw the animal, and cut out both pieces together. Color front and back; glue on whiskers if you choose. Glue together around the edges, leaving a small opening. Stuff some cotton balls inside and then glue closed. Punch a hole in the top of each figure, string with yarn, and then hang your three-dimensional cats from a wooden stick, as shown.

FAMILY LIFE

A WALK ON THE WILD SIDE

Your chances of seeing a bobcat or lynx in the wild are very small. Both species are mostly nocturnal and are very shy and wary; people who spend a great deal of time in the woods often fail to see a single one of these cats, even after many years. However, you may be able to find their tracks. If you live where there's snow, that's the best way to find tracks. Otherwise, mud along streams and ponds is likely to be the best place. The track prints around these pages will help you tell if a track you find belongs to a bobcat or lynx. And while you're looking for tracks, look for places where one of these cats might have a den.

Track prints: Making plaster casts of track prints is easy when you use plaster of Paris (inexpensive, can be purchased at most craft stores). Prepare your plaster, mixing two parts plaster with one part water. To get a good cast, try not to disturb a good fresh print. Just pour your plaster in the print and let it set. When it is dry, pull up on the plaster and gently brush away any snow, dirt, or sand that remains on it. Label it carefully with name of animal, date taken, and place found. Begin a collection of animal track casts. Pretty soon you will be very aware of all the tracks you see on a walk in the woods.

Both cats have their young in the spring in almost any place that offers shelter and protection. Lynx kittens are very small — six or seven ounces. Bobcat kittens are a little larger and may weigh as much as twelve ounces. Both species usually have three to five kittens, but there's one big difference. When snowshoe hares are scarce, the lynx may not have any kittens at all.

Have you ever seen kittens that are just two or three days old? Were their eyes open? Lynx and bobcat kittens have their eyes closed at birth, just like domestic kittens, and they don't open for ten or twelve days. The mother raises her kittens without help from the male and soon teaches them to hunt.

●

Favored Foods

Have you ever watched a cat stalk a mouse or bird in the grass and suddenly pounce on it? That's the way the bobcat usually hunts. It doesn't pursue its prey for a distance the way the lynx does, but prefers to sneak close and then either leap onto its prey or catch it with a quick burst of speed. Besides the usual smaller prey, bobcats will sometimes kill deer in deep snow in their wintering areas. Usually only large male bobcats kill deer; the deer killed are apt to be fawns or bigger deer weakened by disease, injury, or starvation.

Bobcats and lynx both eat mice, birds, and other small prey, but the lynx depends heavily on the snowshoe hare, the big-footed northern hare that turns white in winter. With their long legs and huge, furry feet that act like snowshoes, the lynx is designed to chase and catch the speedy hares. When hares are scarce, lynx may starve. Lynx will also feed on dead deer, but they seldom kill them.

BOBCAT TRACK

AMPHIBIANS

As you'll find out, amphibians are special because they spend part of their lives in water breathing through gills like fish do, and part of their lives above water breathing air through lungs, just as you do. Unlike mammals, though, amphibians are cold-blooded. That means their body temperature goes up or down according to the temperature of the air or water where they live.

One of the nicest things about amphibians — toads, frogs, and salamanders — is that, unlike mammals, they're safe to pick up and handle gently. Look at them closely and then put them down. Please don't try to take them home with you — they need to stay in their own habitat.

LARVA   EFT   NEWT

BABY   KID   ADULT

THE EFT AND THE NEWT

• RANGE MAP •

Have you ever looked into the quiet waters of a pond and seen a small creature that looks something like a tiny, yellowish-brown alligator with small red spots on its back? If you live in the eastern United States or the Maritime Provinces of Canada, you were looking at an *eastern newt,* also called the *red-spotted* newt.

While walking in the woods during or right after a rain, have you seen a similar creature colored orange or red? If so, you probably didn't think it was the very same kind of newt which you saw in the quiet water — but it was! They're two stages of the same creature, just like the tadpole and the frog. How can that be? Well, that requires some understanding of the wonderful ways of newts and their relatives.

FOOD KEY

MOSQUITO LARVAE

FAMILY LIFE

Like other amphibians, newts don't take care of their young. Once they've mated and the females have laid their eggs, they simply swim away and leave them. When the tiny larvae hatch, they're entirely on their own.

A Perfect Word

The word amphibian comes from two Greek words meaning "having a life of two kinds." This tells us a lot about amphibians, and why they're so different from other kinds of creatures. You see, amphibians really do lead two kinds of lives — one as a larva or tadpole which breathes through gills in the water and the other as an adult which breathes air with lungs. But if this seems amazing, consider what newts do. They go through not just two but THREE different stages — larva, eft, and adult newt!

★

Meet the Salamander Family

Newts are members of a larger group called *salamanders*. Salamanders look almost like small lizards, because they have a long tail, a long, slender body, and four short legs. Why aren't salamanders lizards, then?

For one thing, lizards have dry skins, and salamanders have smooth, moist skins. There's another very important difference, too. Salamanders — including newts — belong to a much larger group known as *amphibians,* that includes frogs and toads, while lizards belong to a group known as *reptiles* that includes alligators and crocodiles.

A WALK ON THE WILD SIDE

Go to a quiet pond and try to find some newts. With their four legs and long tail, they look almost like tiny alligators — except that they have short, rounded snouts. Now go into the summer woods right after a rain and look for the orange or red color of the eft. Usually they're quite easy to see because of their color.

See for yourself: There are many other interesting kinds of salamanders besides the newt. These include the spotted salamander, the mudpuppy, the redback, the dusky, the four-toed, and the two-lined salamanders. You may see some of these while you look for the newt and the eft. Try to find out which salamanders live in your area and see as many of them as possible. A good field guide to amphibians, your state wildlife agency, a local natural history museum, or a conservation organization may be able to help you.

See How They Change

In the springtime, the newt's eggs hatch in quiet water and become *larvae* — the first stage after hatching, just as the tadpole is the first stage after frogs' eggs hatch. The larva looks quite a lot like a small adult newt, except that it has *gills*, for breathing under water, that look like feathers sticking out just behind its head. It grows bigger during the summer, and then gradually loses its gills, develops lungs, and becomes an *eft*, the second stage in the life of this amphibian. Can you imagine what an amazing change this is? One day the little creature is breathing through gills, like a fish, and a few days later it's breathing with lungs, just the way you do!

The eft then leaves the water, usually on a rainy night in late summer or autumn, and travels into nearby woods. It looks like an adult newt, except that it's a handsome red or orange. Now it lives underneath logs and rocks, but it often comes out after a rain. That's when you can easily find these brightly colored little creatures.

After spending anywhere from two to seven years in the woods, the efts become mature enough to mate. This is the third stage — the *adult newt*. A full-grown newt isn't very large — only about three and a half inches long. How long is your hand from the tips of your fingers to where it joins your wrist? Depending on your size, your hand may be longer than the whole newt!

One more thing that is very interesting is that the adults return to live the rest of their lives in water, although they continue to breathe air with their lungs. When they return to the water, they also develop a thin, wavy ridge along the top and bottom of the tail and change back to a yellowish-brown color.

Homemade clay salamanders: Here's what you'll need to make a whole group of salamanders in all their varied stages of development:

1 cup cornstarch
1 cup baking soda
1¼ cups cold water
Acrylic paints and paintbrush

Ask a grown-up to help you mix the cornstarch, baking soda, and water in a saucepan over medium heat. Stir the mixture constantly until it is thickened, about 5 minutes. Remove from heat.

When the clay is cool, shape your salamander by rolling a long coil for the body. Shape legs, eyes, and tail. Create as many salamanders as you wish.

Let the clay dry for about 2 days. Then, paint with acrylic paints — either realistically or with great imagination!

ROLL A LONG CLAY COIL FOR THE BODY

MAKE AS MANY AS YOU WISH

HOME SWEET HOME

A New Name

Does the word *newt* seem like a funny word to you? Well, it came about in a funny way. In the early days of the English language, this little salamander was called an *ewt*. Then, perhaps six or seven hundred years ago, an *ewt* was somehow changed to a *newt*. Why do you think that may have happened?

Newts don't have a special spot that they call home, the way many birds and other animals do. Instead, they require different types of *habitat* during their lifetime. Habitat is an area in which something lives — an area big enough to contain everything the creature needs in order to survive, such as food, water, and cover to protect it from enemies. Eastern newts are especially interesting because they move from one habitat to another and back again.

Special changes: Newts are a special amphibian with their *three* different stages in their life. They require different *habitat* during their lifetime, too. Fold a large piece of paper into three parts. Consider the three stages — larva, eft, newt — and draw them in their habitat.

You experience stages in your life as well. Draw yourself and show some of the changes you have made or will make. (Example: Where did you eat as a baby? as a child? as an adult?)

THE COMMON TOAD

FOOD KEY

ANTS

FLIES

SLUGS

SPIDERS

• RANGE MAP •

Pity the poor toad! Toads have had a bad reputation for hundreds — perhaps thousands — of years. It's hard to say why, unless it's their brown, warty appearance. Have you ever read a fairy tale that had a toad in it? Was the toad supposed to be ugly? Toads are nearly always described as ugly in fairy tales, and they were said to be used in witches' brews and other unpleasant things. The truth is that if we forget everything we've been told about how warty and ugly the toad is, we can see that in many ways it's a rather handsome creature — and a very useful and interesting one, too.

Toads are amphibians, like the newt, so they spend part of their lives (the tadpole stage) in water breathing with gills, and part as adults breathing air with lungs, as we do. There are about fifteen different species of toads in North America. Many of these are in the American Southwest — but the *horned toad* isn't one of them! The horned toad is a lizard, and not a toad at all. There are two species of toads in North America that might be called the *common toad* — the *American toad* in the East and the *Western toad* (see range map). They're very similar, so we'll just talk about both species as the common toad.

How can you tell a toad from a frog? Frogs have a smooth skin that is at least slightly moist, while toads have a rough, warty-looking, dry skin. Toads also have shorter legs, better suited to short hops, while the longer-legged frogs can leap much farther.

FAMILY LIFE

Male toads arrive at the mating areas first, early in the spring. There they sing loudly to attract the females. The female toad is a lot bigger than the male, so if you see a really big, fat toad, it's almost certain to be a female. When they mate, the females lay two long strings of jelly-coated eggs. A female toad can lay 3,000 or more eggs each spring. Each of her two egg strings may be more than twelve feet long. Have you ever seen frogs' or toads' eggs in the water? You can tell one type from the other because the frogs' eggs are in a big ball, instead of the strings laid by toads.

Depending on temperature, the eggs hatch in 3 – 12 days. The tadpoles (or toadpoles, as they're sometimes jokingly called) are black, so they're easy to tell from the frog's brownish tadpoles. Like all tadpoles, they soon grow legs, and lose their tails. Then they've become tiny toads less than a half-inch long. It takes about two months for this to happen. These miniature toads move onto land and begin the slow process of becoming full-grown adults, which takes three years.

FROG EGGS

TOAD EGGS

Sing Out

WHAT'S FOR DINNER?

Toads eat a lot of things, such as slugs and earthworms that come above ground, but mostly they eat insects, which makes them very helpful. Their unusual tongues help them in their insect hunting.

Is your tongue hitched at the front or back of your mouth? Like frogs, toads have a tongue hitched at the front of the mouth and that makes it just right for catching insects. When an insect comes within range, the toad flips out its long tongue like lightning, and GLOM! — it's caught the insect on the sticky tip of its tongue!

Toads are quiet for most of the year, but the males sing long and loud during the mating season. Perhaps you've heard their song in the spring. It's a long, high trill that seems to go on and on and may last for thirty seconds. Some other frogs and toads also trill, but their song is much shorter than the common toad's.

Toad trills: Take a deep breath and try to sing a note and hold it just as long as you can without taking a breath. Have someone time you, using a watch with a second hand. Can you hold the note for thirty seconds? That's how long a male toad can hold his note. Isn't it amazing that such a little thing can sing so loudly for so long without stopping?

ORIGAMI HOPPING TOAD

This little jumper is made from a 6" square piece of paper. Leftover gift wrap or paper from a telephone book work well.

1. Place the paper, wrong side up, on the table. Fold it in half, first one way and then the other.

2. Fold each corner to the center. Then fold points A and B so they meet in the middle.

3. Fold the bottom up.

4. Fold A and B in so they meet in the middle at the bottom.

5. Fold the bottom up, about one third of the way. Now fold this piece down in half again.

6. Fold the top point down. Turn over and press your finger down on the toad's back. Slide your finger off and watch your toad hop away!

I.

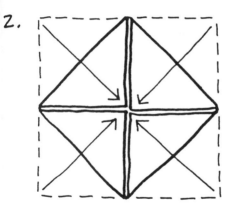

2.

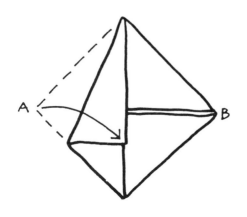

3.

4.

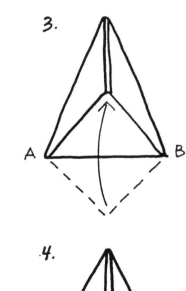

5.

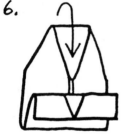

6.

(Adapted from Susan Milord's *The Kids' Nature Book*)

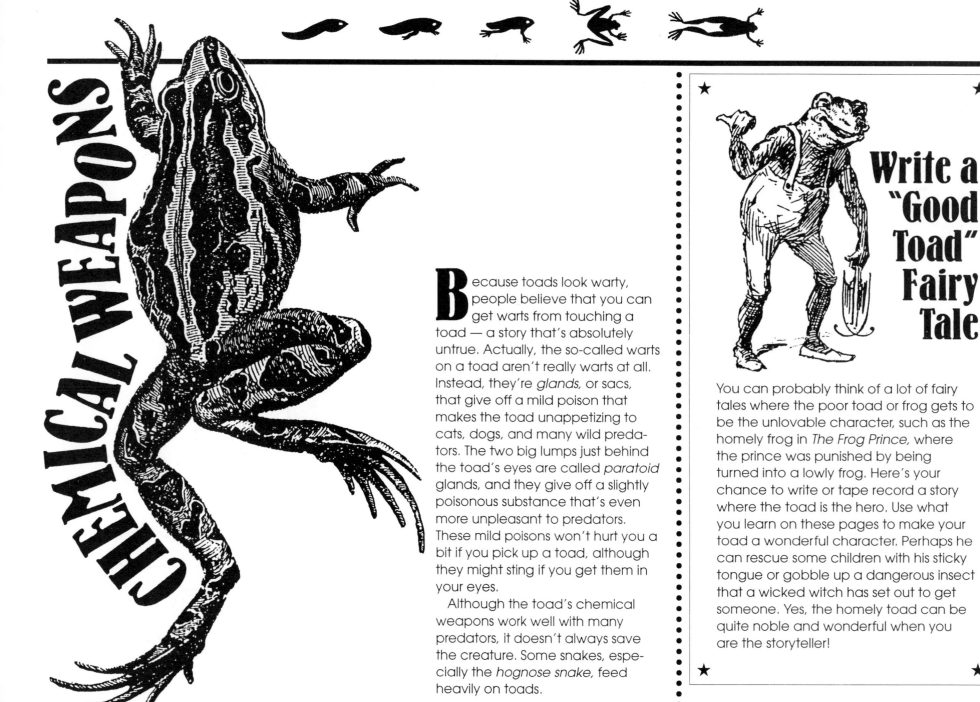

CHEMICAL WEAPONS

Because toads look warty, people believe that you can get warts from touching a toad — a story that's absolutely untrue. Actually, the so-called warts on a toad aren't really warts at all. Instead, they're *glands,* or sacs, that give off a mild poison that makes the toad unappetizing to cats, dogs, and many wild predators. The two big lumps just behind the toad's eyes are called *paratoid* glands, and they give off a slightly poisonous substance that's even more unpleasant to predators. These mild poisons won't hurt you a bit if you pick up a toad, although they might sting if you get them in your eyes.

Although the toad's chemical weapons work well with many predators, it doesn't always save the creature. Some snakes, especially the *hognose snake,* feed heavily on toads.

Write a "Good Toad" Fairy Tale

You can probably think of a lot of fairy tales where the poor toad or frog gets to be the unlovable character, such as the homely frog in *The Frog Prince,* where the prince was punished by being turned into a lowly frog. Here's your chance to write or tape record a story where the toad is the hero. Use what you learn on these pages to make your toad a wonderful character. Perhaps he can rescue some children with his sticky tongue or gobble up a dangerous insect that a wicked witch has set out to get someone. Yes, the homely toad can be quite noble and wonderful when you are the storyteller!

Go to a marsh in the early spring and listen for the singing — or trilling — of the male toad. You won't have much trouble hearing it, because it's quite loud. If you look carefully, you may be able to see the mating toads, with the male clasping the female while she lays her strings of eggs.

After the mating season, search for toads in your yard or in woods and fields. If it isn't too hot and dry, look in and around vegetable or flower gardens, in slightly damp areas, on the shady side of a house, or other places where toads can rest during the daytime — even a flowerpot! You may also find that toads are more active at night during the summer.

It's a lot of fun to find toads — especially the tiny ones. Even though it may be very tempting to take them home to keep in a terrarium, please don't do that. Toads are happiest when they are in their own environment, and they usually get quite sick and die when you attempt to move them.

Brown and gold: Even though you can't take a toad home with you, you can often gently pick one up and study it briefly. See how many different shades of brown it has. Why not paint or color a picture of a toad and try to put in its different shades of brown, as well as the gold around the outer part of the toad's eyes. Draw some of the grass and weeds around it, showing how well the toad is *camouflaged.*

Favorite Toad Stories

Once you've learned to appreciate toads for the cute and clever creatures that they are, you are sure to love Arnold Lobel's wonderful stories about two best friends, a frog and a toad. Begin with *Frog and Toad Are Friends* and then read the whole series. They are available in paperback. And don't overlook Kenneth Graham's wonderful book, *The Wind in the Willows,* which features the pompous, bragging Mr. Toad as a main character.

HOME SWEET HOME

For most of the year, toads live on land. They aren't fussy where they live, either. Common toads can be found in fields, forests, people's gardens and yards, damp areas, high mountainsides — just about anywhere. Do you have a toad living under your porch or front or back steps? Toads often hide in such cool, shady places during the heat of the day and then come out at night.

Toads return to water only during the spring mating season. Then you can find them in large numbers in swamps and quiet areas along the shores of ponds.

It's Just Water!

Have you ever picked up a toad and had it wet all over your hand? Most people assume the toad is urinating, but it isn't. It's really releasing pure water stored in its body to keep it from becoming too dry. No one is quite sure why the toad releases this water when it's frightened, but it may be some kind of defense mechanism. Did it scare you enough to put the toad down?

BIRDS

Birds are wonderful for many reasons, but perhaps the most fascinating thing about them is that almost all of them can fly. Isn't it fun to watch how swiftly and gracefully birds fly, and to see how different the flight of, say, a swallow is from that of an owl? We also enjoy birds because of the beautiful songs which many of them sing, as well as their bright colors.

There's one other reason why birds are very special. You probably thought that all the dinosaurs were extinct. Well, most of them are, but one kind of dinosaur evolved into a bird, so birds are really the direct descendants of the dinosaurs! Scientists have even found fossils of the creature — *Archaeopteryx* — that links birds and dinosaurs. It was like a dinosaur in many ways, but had wings and feathers like a modern bird. Now isn't *that* exciting?

Like mammals, birds are warm-blooded and care for their young, although they don't produce milk to feed them. Of course, birds have feathers instead of hair.

OWLS

FOOD KEY

MICE

RABBITS

BIRD

Owls can be found throughout North America. They occupy a variety of habitat, from the frigid waters of the Arctic Tundra to the sunny climates of Florida and the southwestern United States, and from deep forests to open desert and grasslands. This means that at least one species of owl lives wherever you live in North America, and most likely, you have several species near you.

NATURALLY SPEAKING

There are twelve different species of owls in North America, and they're alike in many ways. They all have facial disks and fixed eyes at the front of their heads, for instance, but they share some other traits, as well. They look much larger than they really are because their feathers are so fluffy, but owls are really quite small. Did you know that owls, even large ones, hardly make a sound when they fly? They can fly so silently because of their very wide wings and the soft edges of their flight feathers. Silent flight is a great adaptation, because it keeps mice and other prey from hearing the owl's approach.

A WALK ON THE WILD SIDE

Go out in the woods in the spring or fall when the leaves are off and look for places where owls might nest. Can you find woodpecker holes and natural cavities in trees? What about old nests of large birds, such as crows or hawks? Do you see any owl pellets on the ground? If you were an owl, how easy would it be for you to find a nesting place?

How Wise Is the Owl?

We speak of being "*as wise as an owl*," but most scientists don't think owls are very smart — not as smart as crows and ravens, for instance. So why do people think owls are wise? It's probably because they have large, immoveable, round eyes in the front of their faces (penguins are the only other birds with eyes at the front). Also, owls have a *facial disk* — very short feathers arranged in a rounded pattern on the front of their heads. This facial disk and the staring eyes in front sometimes make owls look almost human — and wise!

Wise eyes: These pinecone owls have wise, wide eyes, and they're a lot of fun to make. If you live in a place where there aren't pinecones, you can buy them at most craft stores.

Here's what you'll need:

Light-colored felt scraps
Scissors, glue
Pinecones
Buttons

Cut two 1" circles from the felt to make eyes. Glue the buttons onto the felt circles to make a pupil for each eye. Glue eyes to the front of a pinecone to create a face. Make a beak by cutting a triangle from the felt; glue triangle on upside down. Make as many owls as you wish; then arrange them on a windowsill or bookshelf. (If the pinecones don't stand, you may want to glue them to a paper plate or make a base out of clay.)

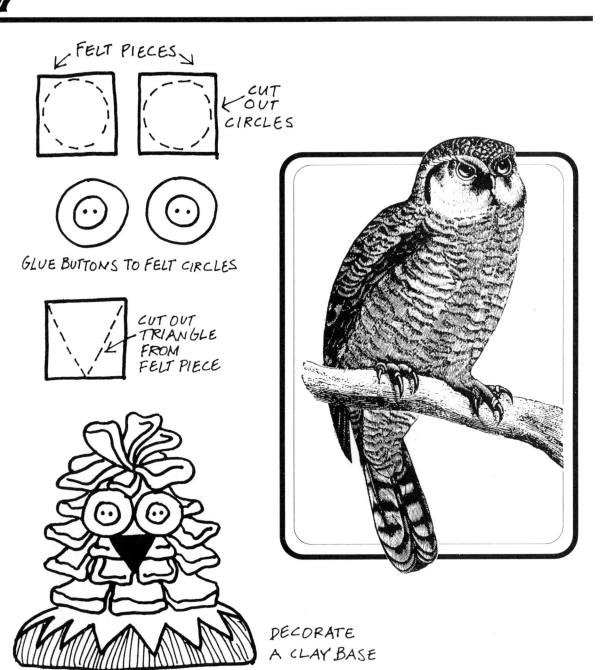

FELT PIECES

CUT OUT CIRCLES

GLUE BUTTONS TO FELT CIRCLES

CUT OUT TRIANGLE FROM FELT PIECE

DECORATE A CLAY BASE

The Better to See You with!

Because owls are out mostly at night, many people think they're almost blind in the daytime. Actually, owls can see quite well in daylight; the reason they fly mostly at night is because that's when most of their prey is out, and owls have hearing, eyesight, and flight wonderfully adapted to night hunting.

An owl can't move its eyes, but it makes up for it by being able to turn its head up to three-quarters of the way around — and it can do it so fast you can hardly see it happen. It's a funny experience to be staring at an owl's face and suddenly find yourself looking at the back of its head!

Owl-sight: Wait until it's almost too dark to see outdoors and then look through a pair of good binoculars. Does everything seem a little brighter, so that you can see better? That's because binoculars collect more light than your eyes. But even with high-powered binoculars, your eyes don't come close to seeing as well in the dark as an owl's eyes. An owl's eyes are 100 times as sensitive to light as our human eyes are. Is it any wonder they can see so well at night?

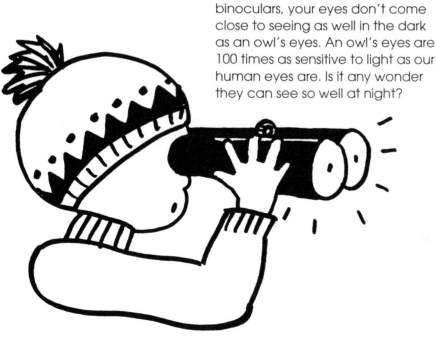

And, the Better to Hear You with

Some owls seem to have ears that stick up above their heads like a dog's or cat's ears. Although these are called *ear tufts,* they're really nothing but soft feathers. Owls have amazing hearing, but they don't have ears we can see.

Most creatures have two ears that are almost the same, but an owl's two ears are quite different from each other. Because one ear hears sounds from above better, and the other sounds from below, an owl can locate the height of its prey extremely well by sound alone. Also, by tiny differences in the time a sound reaches each ear, the owl can tell just where its prey is from right to left.

Although owls have amazing night vision, they hunt more by sound than by sight. One owl expert says that some owls can hear a mouse squeak a half mile away!

The mouse that roared: Get a toy mouse or other toy animal that squeaks when you squeeze it. Go outdoors and have someone walk slowly away from you while squeaking the toy. Stop the person as soon as you can't hear the squeak anymore. How far away could you hear the squeak? Now have someone show you how far away a half mile is. Can you imagine hearing a squeak that far away?

FUN FACTS

Owls have an unusual digestive system. They eat small prey whole — bones, fur, and all. The parts that can't be used for food (fur, bones, feathers) are packed together into *pellets* — small, rather hard, rounded objects. Then they *regurgitate* (re-GUR-ji-tate) the pellets. That mean's bringing them up from their stomachs much the way you throw up when you're sick — except that it's natural and not unpleasant for the owl. If you find lots of owl pellets under a tree in the woods, it's a tree where an owl often roosts.

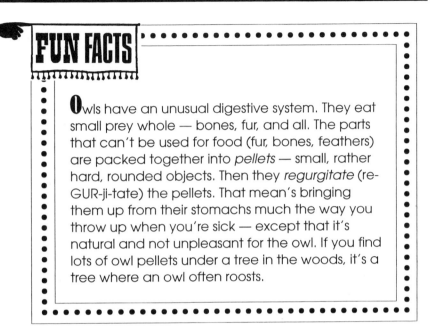

Birds of a Different Feather

Although owls have these and other things in common, they also come in all sizes, shapes, and varied habits — just like human beings do. Now that we know some of their similarities, let's look at four North American owls to see how different they can be. To make it easier to understand these differences, let's make a chart comparing characteristics.

Chart it: Charts help people organize, compare, and remember information. You can make a chart in a lot of different ways depending on the kind of data, or information, you have. Maybe you like to use words and numbers, or maybe you like to use drawings or symbols. Make a chart that works for you. Here is one way to set it up, but you don't have to do the same. Draw it on a piece of graph paper, lined paper, or plain paper.

Using data: For this chart, we have data on four types of North American owls. List the kinds of owls across the top of your chart and list the characteristics we will focus on down the side — size, wing span, number and color of eggs, home (nest), food, and range.

The Barred Owl:
Size: medium-large weighing about 1½ lbs.
Wing span: 3½ feet
Eggs: 2 – 4 white eggs in spring
Nest: tree hollow or old crow's nest
Food: small prey — mice, frogs, large insects
Range: eastern North America; central Canada

The Great Horned Owl:
Size: one of largest at 2½ – 3 lbs.
Wing span: about 5 feet
Eggs: 2 – 3 white eggs in January!
Nest: old crow or hawk's nest
Food: crows, rabbits, skunks, mice
Range: nearly all North America

The Snowy Owl:
Size: heaviest owl at 4½ lbs.
Wing span: about 5 feet
Eggs: 5 – 8 white eggs
Nest: feathers in ground — no trees in habitat
Food: lemmings, Arctic hares, ptarmigan
Range: northern United States; all of Canada

The Saw-whet Owl:
Size: smallest at 3 ounces and 7 inches
Wing span: about 17 inches
Eggs: 3 – 4 white eggs
Nest: old woodpecker hole or tree hole
Food: mice, small squirrels, large insects
Range: most of North America except southcentral U.S. and northern Canada

★

Now that you've done your owl chart, what do you realize about a chart? Does it help you organize and compare information? Can you easily tell which owl is biggest? smallest? has most eggs? Can you tell interesting details? How might you include details such as the fact that the tiny saw-whet owl is a great mouser because its tiny talons are strong and sharp as needles, or that when the lemmings — which are the snowy owl's favorite food — aren't plentiful, some of these owls leave their arctic range and move south into northern United States? Maybe you would like to add some of the data to your chart from the section, "Give a Hoot."

★

TYPE OF OWL:	BARRED OWL	GREAT HORNED OWL	SNOWY OWL	SAW-WHET OWL
SIZE:				
WING SPAN:				
EGGS:				
NEST:				
FOOD:				
OTHER:				

Give a Hoot!

Have you ever heard an owl hoot? It can be an eerie sound in the darkness, and when we think of owls, we think of hooting. That's natural, because hooting is a common sort of owl call. But, as you'll see, owls make many other kinds of sounds, some of them very strange — and there are species of owls that don't hoot at all!

For example, barred owls are very talkative and often can be heard calling in the late afternoon. Their best-known call is a series of eight hoots, *hooohooohooHOOO hooohooohooHOOOaww,* which gives this owl its nickname of "Eight Hooter." However, barred owls make a lot of other noises, including a loud scream and another call that sounds strangely similar to some kinds of monkeys — a rapid series of hoohoohawhaw ahhahhahhahhahhah. The Great Horned Owl only hoots occasionally — but it is a deep, loud hoot that can be heard for great distances. The Snowy Owl and Saw-whet Owl are rarely heard, except perhaps during mating season.

★ MOUSE PATROL ★

Just about everyone enjoys seeing owls, and with good reason. Owls are fascinating birds, and we don't see them very often because they usually aren't active in the daylight. But owls weren't always so popular. They used to have a bad reputation in the days when most farmers kept chickens. Every now and then a large owl would learn how easy it was to kill and eat hens at dawn or dusk — and sometimes right in broad daylight. Nowadays, however, we know that owls do far more good than harm by controlling the population of mice, voles, rats, lemmings, and other small rodents. In fact, a pair of barn owls with young owls to feed will catch from 20 – 30 mice a night.

NATIVE AMERICAN LEGENDS

The Iroquois of the Northeastern United States and Southeastern Canada explained the owl's unusual looks with this fine story.

■

Raweno, the maker of the world, was giving the rabbit what it wanted — long ears and long, strong hind legs. The owl was waiting its turn and watching, all the while telling Raweno the many things it wanted, such as a long neck and beautiful red feathers.

Raweno ordered the owl to close its eyes, because no one was allowed to watch Raweno do his work. When the owl refused, Raweno became very angry. He grabbed the owl and stuffed its neck down into its body. Then he shook the owl so hard that its eyes grew big and round with fright. Finally, Raweno commanded the owl to sleep in the daytime and hunt at night, and since then the owl has hunted at night and has big eyes and almost no neck.

■

Write a Poem about Owls

Making up your own poem is a wonderful and creative way to express your love for wild creatures. Even if you've never seen an owl with your own eyes, you can still create a poem about one, because poetry allows your imagination to run wild.

When making up your poem, think of words that create a feeling or a picture. The words in a poem don't have to rhyme — unless you choose to write a poem in rhyme. Here's a short poem to get you started, and then it's your turn.

A Walk in the Woods
by Me
In the woods, up in a tree,
a bird is staring, wide-eyed, at me.
She has white feathers,
no neck and a beak.
I call to her softly,
she lets out a screech!

THE HERON

FOOD KEY

FISH

FROGS

SALAMANDERS

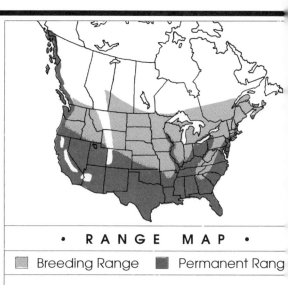

• R A N G E   M A P •

☐ Breeding Range   ■ Permanent Rang...

Note: *There is no winter range shown because the herons that breed in the north only fly south into the permanent range in winter.*

People often make the mistake of calling herons — especially *great blue herons* — cranes. Yes, herons look a lot like cranes, with their long legs and necks, but the two are really quite different. In fact, no matter how much they may look alike, they aren't even closely related!

The sandhill and whooping cranes are the only cranes native to North America. It's a different story with herons, though. There are more than a dozen North American members of the heron family, in all different sizes and colors. Because of its large size, it's the great blue heron which is most often confused with cranes, so let's look at this heron and the two cranes to see the ways in which they're quite different, as well as ways in which they're similar.

Enormous, Graceful Birds

Have you ever seen a great, long-legged, long-necked bird wading in quiet water, striding across a grain field, or flying majestically overhead? If you have, you were looking at a heron or crane.

The great blue heron stands about four feet tall and has a wingspan of nearly six feet. The sandhill crane is about the same size, and the whooping crane is even larger with a wingspan of seven and a half feet. Standing at nearly five feet high, the whooper is also the tallest bird in North America!

AND THE CRANE

Old Timers

Cranes are very ancient as birds go. The earliest crane fossils, which were found in North America, go back forty or fifty million years. That's only fifteen to twenty-five million years after the dinosaurs died out — and that's really ancient!

FOOD KEY

FISH

FROGS

GRAIN

GRASSES

• RANGE MAP •

Breeding Range   Permanent Range
Winter Range

The Great Migration

The sandhill crane nests across northern Canada and Alaska, as well as near the western Great Lakes. In the fall, these great birds *migrate,* or move, in huge flocks to winter in Arizona, Texas, and southern California. Most of the wild whooping cranes left in the world nest in Wood Buffalo State Park in the Mackenzie district of northern Canada, migrating as a flock, in the fall, to the Aransas Wildlife Refuge on the Gulf coast of Texas.

This is quite different from the great blue heron, which, if it migrates at all, flies alone and often only goes far enough south to find water that doesn't freeze in the winter.

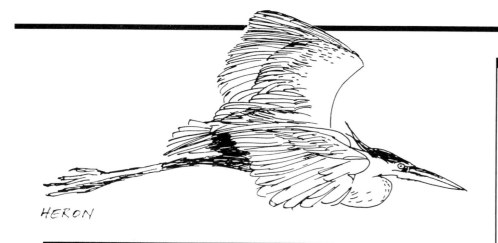

HERON

Which One Am I?

Telling the two cranes from the great blue heron really isn't very difficult, once you know what to look for. Standing still, the two cranes show a nice red patch on the front of the face (use the Cree legend about the crane as a memory helper), while the heron doesn't have any red at all.

The birds' appearance in flight is another clear, distinguishing characteristic. Cranes fly with their long necks straight out, but the blue heron folds its neck back and flies with its head almost on its shoulders.

CRANE

NATIVE AMERICAN LEGENDS

The Crees are a native people who live in northern Canada near James Bay and the Saskatchewan River. According to them, this is how the crane got its long legs.

■

The rabbit wanted to ride on the moon, but he couldn't fly and needed a bird to carry him. None of the birds wanted to take the rabbit on this difficult journey, but finally the crane agreed to do it. The rabbit held onto the crane's legs while they traveled to the moon and back, and the rabbit's weight stretched the crane's legs. The rabbit was so pleased with the crane that, as a gift, he gave the crane the bright red patch of skin on its head.

■

A WALK ON THE WILD SIDE

Try to see some great blue herons. Wildlife refuges, bird sanctuaries, or any places with marshes or shallow, still water are apt to have one or more of these great birds. Don't expect to get very close to them, though — great blue herons are wary and usually fly away at the first sign of an approaching human.

Try to find a heronry (heron rookery). Your state wildlife agency or a local bird club may be able to help you. It's great fun to see the huge nests with the tall herons perched on them. Don't try to get too close, because too much disturbance could interfere with the herons' nesting.

The Flight of the Wild Whooping Crane

The whooping crane's migration certainly covers a lot of territory! Cranes, of course, don't have maps to follow, but you can make a *topographic map* — one that shows mountains and lakes — that will help you to see how far this magnificent bird flies and the type of country it travels over.

Here's what you'll need:

Sheet of white poster board or large piece of cardboard

Pencil, glue, long piece of bright yarn

Map of the United States and Canada
(a large road atlas is good for this)

Homemade dough (see page 153 for recipe)

Tempera paints (blue, brown, green, black),
small paper cups

Paintbrushes

Small pinecones, pine needles, tiny pebbles

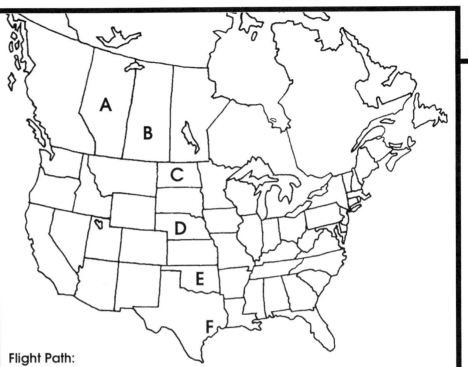

Flight Path:

A *The flock leaves Wood Buffalo National Park (Alberta, Canada).*

B *Fly across the border into Saskatchewan.*

C *Head south and then east into North Dakota.*

D *Follow the flock south into South Dakota, Nebraska, central Kansas.*

E *Fly south into Oklahoma.*

F *Cross the Red River into Texas, flying south to Aransas National Wildlife Refuge on the Gulf coast of Texas.*

Before you begin, cover work surface with old newspaper, and put on a paint smock or old work shirt. Draw a *rough* outline of North America. Use the dough to create lakes and mountains that the crane might see as it follows the "flight plan." Let dough dry; paint the lakes, mountains, and land. Pinecones, pine needles, and pebbles can be glued onto the map for added textures. Glue a piece of yarn along the flight path.

FAMILY LIFE

HERON NEST

HOME SWEET HOME

Great blue herons nest in colonies. This means that the nests are quite close to each other — often only a few feet apart. A number of nests may even be built in a single large tree. These colonies are called *heronries* or *rookeries*. Heron nests are usually in trees and are made of a platform of sticks, lined with softer materials such as reeds and grass.

Unlike great blue herons, both sandhill and whooping cranes nest on the ground in marshy areas. Their nests are mounds built up out of marsh plants. Also unlike herons, the cranes nest singly, rather than in colonies.

Build a nest: Build a great blue heron's nest. Think what you've learned about the way the heron builds its nest. What will you make the base from, and what will you line it with? If you'd like, make some papier-mache eggs to fill the nest. Think about the size of the great blue heron. How big a nest will it take for a bird that large?

Cranes perform a spectacular mating dance. The male and female face each other and then leap off the ground, with their wings, legs, and feet pointed at each other. Then they bow and repeat the whole performance many times, often croaking at each other.

Herons lay three to five greenish-blue eggs. The baby herons are downy, gawky, and homely at first, with their long legs and beaks. The young herons grow rapidly, though, and are ready to leave the nest after about two months.

Cranes lay only two eggs in their nests. These eggs are light brown, with dark spots or blotches. Whooping cranes raise only one of their two young. The larger, stronger one survives, but the smaller one almost never lives. Either the parents give most of the food to the larger chick, or the larger one pecks the smaller one to death or drives it out of the nest. Once out of the nest, the chick will be caught by hungry predators.

CRANE NEST

 **WHAT'S FOR DINNER?**

People confuse what herons and cranes eat. Herons are properly noted for being great fishermen, but cranes eat a much wider variety of food. Although cranes eat fish and frogs, too, — as well as almost any other small creature they can gobble up — they also eat a great deal of grain and tender shoots of grass.

Did you ever hear the expression, "You are what you eat"? Because of their diet of grain and grass, especially when migrating, sandhill cranes taste good and are legally hunted for food by humans. Herons, which are NOT legal to hunt, would taste strong, fishy, and unpleasant because of the food they eat.

It takes a lot of food for great blue herons to feed themselves and their young,

but the adult herons are very good indeed at catching fish, frogs, and other water creatures. Herons will stand still as a statue in one spot for many minutes, patiently waiting for their prey to come along. At other times, they'll stalk very, very slowly and carefully through shallow water, grabbing fish and frogs with a lightning stab of their long bills.

Cranes aren't as slow, patient fishermen as herons, but they have the advantage of eating more kinds of food. Usually they stalk about on their long legs, picking up whatever they can find to eat — insects, mice, fish, grain, frogs, grass, and many other things.

Fishing heron-style: Find a place where there is shallow, still water. Ask a grown-up to go wading with you (please don't go alone). If possible, pick a place where there are small fish, frogs, crayfish, and other aquatic creatures that herons might eat. Wade in the water and pretend you're a heron looking for food. Stand perfectly still in one spot, waiting for food to come to you. You mustn't move! Have someone time you with a watch. When

you're tired of standing in one spot, find out how long you've been there. Do you think a heron could be more patient and wait in one spot for a longer time than you can?

Now move very slowly and carefully through the water. Use your hand as the heron would its long bill, and try to catch something a heron would like to eat. Is it easy? Do you think you're as quick as a heron?

How Do You Know That?

Scientists learn much about birds by being able to track their movement. Birds are banded so that researchers can gather information. Contact your local Audubon Society to learn more about banding.

THREATENED, ENDANGERED, OR EXTINCT

If a species (of animal or plant) is gone forever — like the dinosaurs — it is said to be *extinct*. A species that is *endangered* is in immediate danger of becoming extinct. A population that is *threatened* has so few left that unless action is taken to protect it, the species could become endangered and be near to *extinction*.

THREATENED → ENDANGERED → EXTINCT

LOW POPULATION

NEED IMMEDIATE ATTENTION

GONE FOREVER

Environmentally Yours

Do you know what *extinct* means? It means a species is gone forever — that, like the dinosaurs, it will never be seen again. The magnificent whooping crane is still in great danger of extinction, in spite of the best efforts of biologists for nearly fifty years (sandhill cranes are very plentiful). The whooper's chances of survival have improved, though. In 1941, there were only 16 whooping cranes left in the entire world. By 1993, there were 237, although many of them were cranes raised in captivity.

Raising wild birds and mammals in captivity is something that most people should never do. However, trained experts — biologists and other scientists — can sometimes help endangered species by giving nature a hand and raising the species in captivity. That's the case with the whooping crane.

As these captive whooper flocks increase, some of the cranes are being carefully released into the wild. Biologists hope they'll mate and start new flocks there. Twelve whooping cranes were released in Florida at the start of 1993, for example. The largest whooping crane flock is still the original wild one — now 135 birds — which winters at the Aransas Refuge.

Plan a visit: If you live where sandhill cranes migrate or winter in large flocks, try to see some of them. If you live or plan to travel near the Aransas Refuge on the Gulf coast of Texas, visit it in the winter to see the whooping cranes.

What's Taking So Long?

Why has it taken so many years to restore these great birds? Because cranes don't mate until they're five or six years old, and they only raise one young crane each year. Some of these die before they're old enough to mate. At that rate, a pair of cranes may have to live eight to ten years just to produce two young cranes which live to replace the parents when they die from accidents, disease, or old age. When a creature has so few young, biologists say that it has a very low *reproductive rate.*

How many; how fast: Make a list of creatures that you think have a low reproductive rate (very few young each year, or even every two or three years) and some others which have high reproductive rates. Think about all kinds of living things — insects such as a grasshopper; amphibians like the frog or salamander; reptiles such as snakes and turtles; fish; different kinds of birds, large and small; and mammals from bears to mice. Use this book and an encyclopedia to help you in your investigation.

Get Involved!

Loss and damage to habitat are primary reasons for species to become threatened. Are there any species of animals or plants like the whooping crane that live in your state that are endangered or threatened? Contact your state or provincial wildlife agency or local wildlife conservancy for information. Create a poster to remind yourself and others of some of the species that fall into these categories. Create a Wildlife Watch Club in your neighborhood, class, school, church, or synagogue, or write an article for your local newspaper. You can make a difference by helping others to become more aware. The more people know, the better.

ENDANGERED SPECIES

THE CROW

You've seen crows, haven't you? These good-sized black birds are so common that just about everybody in North America has seen them at one time or another. Ravens aren't as common or widespread (see the range maps), but they've become more numerous in recent years.

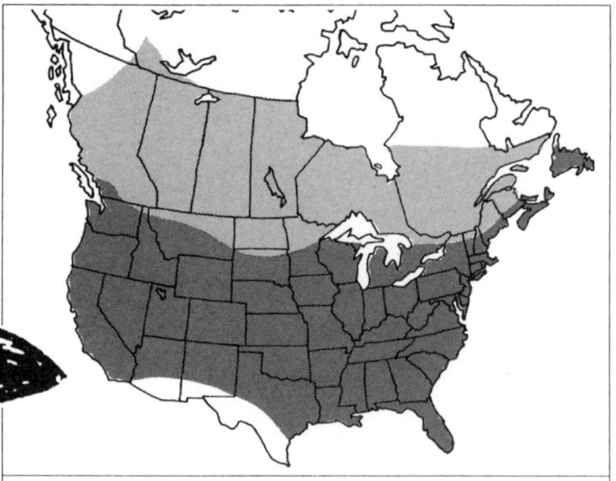

RANGE MAP

■ Breeding Range   ■ Permanent Range

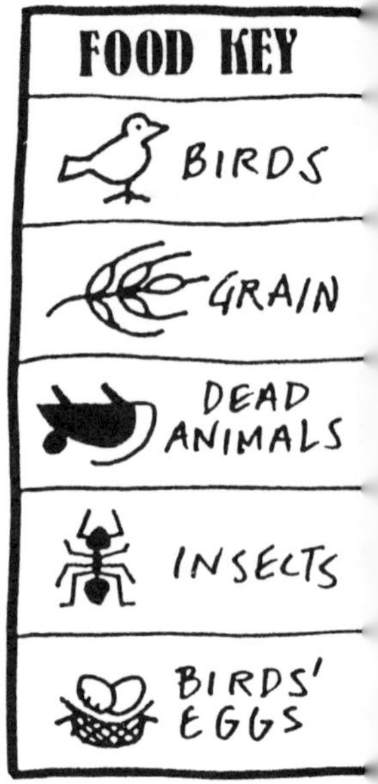

FOOD KEY

🐦 BIRDS

🌾 GRAIN

🐀 DEAD ANIMALS

🐜 INSECTS

🥚 BIRDS' EGGS

Crows and ravens are closely related and look a lot alike, but, as you'll see, there are many differences. If you live where there are both crows and ravens, you can learn to tell these look-alike birds apart. Making the chart of similarities and differences (see page 146) will help you distinguish crows from ravens from now on.

Crows and ravens have a reputation for being very intelligent, and even some scientists agree with this idea. The trouble is that no one — including scientists — really knows for sure, because no scientific studies of these interesting birds' intelligence have been done. We can hope that research will some day tell us whether or not crows and ravens are as smart as many people think.

HOME SWEET HOME

AND THE RAVEN

Just as crows and ravens look much alike, so do their eggs. Both species lay from four to seven dull greenish eggs with dark brown spots. The nests in which the eggs are laid are similar, too — a mass of sticks lined with soft materials, such as feathers, grass, or fur. Crows and ravens don't build their nests in the same places, though. Ravens place their nests on the side of a cliff or in the top of a tall evergreen tree, such as a spruce. Crows, on the other hand, build their nests lower down in trees, where they're more protected.

Build a nest: Build a nest the way you think a crow or raven would build it. Go out in the woods or your yard and pick up plenty of small twigs and sticks. Weave these together to make the main part of the nest, and make it big enough for a bird the size of a crow or raven. Leave a hollowed out area in the center and line it with soft material, such as feathers or fine, dry grass. In the fall when small birds have abandoned their nests, see if you can find an old, *abandoned* nest of a smaller bird, like robins, sparrows, or swallows. How does your crow or raven nest compare in size with theirs? When you're finished, place your nest in the low branches of a tree or in a tall bush.

· RANGE MAP ·

◾ Permanent Range

Wonderful Wings

Construct a bird to hang from your bedroom ceiling.

Here's what you'll need:

Large brown paper grocery bag
Markers, assorted colors
4 straight sticks or dowels, 6" long
Clear tape, hole punch
Heavy string, two 3' pieces

Cut open the paper bag and lay it flat on a table. Fold it in half and draw half of an outline of a bird on it. Cut out the double thickness of the bird. Open up and decorate with markers. Use bright colors; it doesn't have to be black like a crow or raven. Attach the dowels with a few strips of tape as shown. Punch a hole at the tip of each wing, and reinforce them with tape. Tie each end of the string through the holes. If you have permission to hang the bird with its wings outspread from the ceiling, place tacks a few feet apart and attach wing strings, so bird hangs mid-air as if gliding across your room.

Join the Flock

WHAT'S FOR DINNER?

Crows and ravens eat nearly everything — insects, grain, dead animals, birds' eggs and baby birds, garbage, and just about anything else they can find. (What animal does that remind you of?) Ravens are larger than crows, though, and have much more powerful beaks, so they'll try to kill larger prey than crows will tackle.

One farmer heard ravens making a great racket in his pasture. After they had kept it up for several hours, he went to investigate and found the ravens swooping down at a badly confused young fox barely old enough to be out of its den. The ravens flew away when the farmer approached, and the young fox escaped into the woods. However, it seems likely that the ravens would have worn out the little fox and killed it if the farmer hadn't appeared.

Crows have never been very popular with many farmers. Large flocks of crows can certainly do a lot of damage to crops grown near roosting areas. On the other hand, crows eat huge quantities of insects that damage crops, so on the whole, they probably do more good than harm.

Crows are very social birds, and by late fall or early winter they may migrate in flocks for several hundred miles to gather with other flocks at a *roosting area*. These roosting areas are wooded and may have from a few hundred to perhaps as many as a MILLION (1,000,000) crows. Can you imagine how many crows that is? Here's something that may help you. Count out a hundred of something — toothpicks, pennies, or other small objects. Does that seem like a lot? Well, it would take TEN THOUSAND (10,000) piles just like your pile of one hundred in order to make a million! That's a lot of crows, isn't it?

The crows perch in the trees in the roosting area at night and then fly out into the surrounding country to feed during the day. They may have to fly twenty miles or more from large roosting areas in order to find food.

Ravens usually travel in pairs or very small groups. You aren't likely to see ravens in large flocks, like crows.

HOW BIG IS BIG

Ravens are from 22 – 27 inches long from the tip of the beak to the tip of the tail. Crows run from 17 – 21 inches long. A large crow is nearly the same size as a small raven, and that's why telling the two apart just by size is often difficult. Do you have a yardstick? If you do, compare how long crows and ravens are.

17 – 21 INCHES

22 – 27 INCHES

FAMILY LIFE

A mated pair of crows often has several younger crows with it, and these younger birds help to build nests and feed the baby crows, much the way younger wolves in the pack help the alpha wolves raise their young.

The mother raven has to incubate her eggs for about three weeks before they hatch, while the crow's eggs take about three days less to hatch. After hatching, young crows are ready to leave the nest when they're about three and a half weeks old. Young ravens take consider-ably longer — nearly six weeks — before they can fly from the nest.

At-a-glance chart: One way to really under-stand closely related animals such as the crow and the raven is to make a list of all their *similarities*, or things that are alike, and a list of their *differences*, or things that aren't alike. Set up your chart on a piece of paper as shown with two columns under differences. Either write in similarities and differences as you come across them, or record them with symbols or pictures.

NATIVE AMERICAN LEGENDS

As you listen to the various American Indian legends about wildlife in this book, you'll begin to see a pattern of how the Native Americans viewed wildlife with great wonder, interest, and respect. According to the Brule Sioux, who were buffalo hunters of the northern plains, all crows were once white. Here is their tale:

■

People depended on the buffalo for food, but the crows flew down and warned the buffalo whenever the Indians planned to hunt them. Because they could no longer kill any buffalo, the Indians began to starve.

Finally, an Indian disguised himself with a buffalo skin and went among the buffalo. When the crows came to warn the buffalo, they all fled, except for the disguised Indian. Then the Great Crow, the leader of the crows, landed on the back of the disguised Indian to warn him, and the Indian quickly seized the crow.

When the Indian brought the crow back to the Council Fire, an angry Indian hunter threw the crow into the fire. The crow escaped, but not before his feathers had been blackened — and crows have been black ever since!

■

Make a Glider

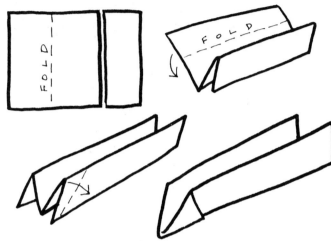

The raven's glide is much like a paper airplane. Another animal that has an amazing glide is the flying squirrel who can glide at least 100 feet. Want to have some great fun? Make your favorite paper airplane or the one described below, stand on a chair for added height, aim your plane upwards, and launch. Notice how smoothly a good launch will glide — just like a raven. How far does it glide? Get a measuring tape to check. Remember: 1 foot = 12 inches; 3 feet = 1 yard. Compare your distances with a friend's.

1. Find a piece of 8½" x 11" paper.

2. Fold the top edge down, dividing the paper into thirds. Cut away the bottom third.

3. Holding the remaining piece, which is already folded in half, take a loose corner and fold it down to the edge with the crease. Repeat on the other side.

4. Take the top edge of each side and fold down to the creased edge.

Read a Poem

Crows can be taught to imitate a few human sounds, but they're not very good at it. Parrots and mynahs are much better at this sort of thing. Ravens are even poorer than crows at mimicking humans. Edgar Allen Poe wrote a famous poem called "The Raven," in which a raven keeps saying, "Nevermore." A man who had a pet raven thought it would be fun to teach the bird to say, "Nevermore." He succeeded, too — but it took him six whole years to teach the raven that one word!

LET'S TALK ABOUT IT

Just about everyone knows what crows sound like. Their *caw, caw, caw* is so familiar that we often don't even notice it. Cawing is about the only sound that crows make, but ravens are a very different story.

Ravens make a great variety of sounds, but the most common are a harsh *crrroak* and a ringing, wooden *goink* that sounds almost as if someone had hit a huge wooden gong. Ravens also make noises that, at a distance, sound almost like people talking and laughing. The differences in voices is one of the best ways to tell crows and ravens apart.

Flying High

Crows and ravens fly very differently, so they're usually easy to tell apart in the air. Crows fly steadily — flop, flop, flop — and seldom glide except in a strong wind or when landing. But ravens are marvelous fliers. They aren't fast, like a peregrine falcon, but they can do wonderful maneuvers, much like a stunt pilot in a small, slow airplane.

Ravens often glide or soar like hawks, without flapping their wings. At other times they'll bank, dive, drop like a plane that's lost its engine, or do rolls and other tricky maneuvers. Sometimes they'll even swoop at each other and tumble around together in the air in make-believe fights! There are very few birds that can match the raven's fancy flying.

TWO FALCONS THE PEREGRINE AND THE KESTREL

FOOD KEY

GRASSHOPPERS

BIRDS

Falcons are the glamour birds among hawks. Swift and beautiful in flight, they're streamlined, with pointed wings and rather long tails. You might consider them the fighter planes of the bird world. Two of the handsomest falcons are the peregrine and the kestrel, which is commonly called the sparrow hawk.

KESTREL

PEREGRINE

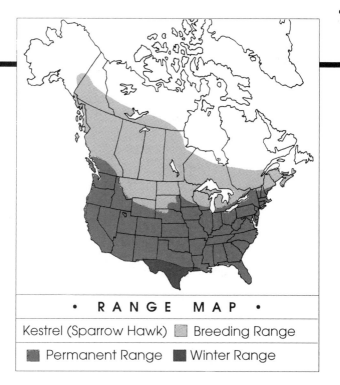

• R A N G E   M A P •

| Kestrel (Sparrow Hawk) | Breeding Range |
| Permanent Range | Winter Range |

Hunting Grounds

Both the peregrine and the kestrel are birds of open country, where most of their prey lives, rather than of heavily forested areas. The kestrel, especially, likes open farm country, where you can see it perching on telephone and electric wires, or on the small branches of dead trees.

The kestrel's nickname, "sparrow hawk" causes most people to think it feeds mainly on small birds. Kestrels do occasionally catch a small bird, as well as some mice and voles, but their main food supply is insects. They don't feed on tiny insects like mosquitoes, of course, but spend most of their time catching large insects such as grasshoppers, crickets, and beetles.

Two Beautiful Birds

The peregrine is a fierce-looking bird about the size of a crow. Its upper parts are a slate gray, while the underside is light colored with small, dark spots or short stripes. A dark, pointed band comes down from the eye to the bottom part of the head. Seen from the front, these bands look like long, drooping mustaches.

The little kestrel is the smallest of all North American hawks, as well as the most beautiful. Only about the size of a robin or blue jay, the kestrel is a lovely rusty red, with black, white, and gray markings around the face and head. The female has rusty wings, too, but the male's are slate gray. Like the peregrine, the kestrel appears to have long, drooping black mustaches.

As with other hawks, the female peregrine and kestrel are quite a lot larger than the males — sometimes as much as a third larger.

Listen and draw: Often when someone is describing something, we let our thoughts drift off, but description is very important. Listen again to the description of the peregrine and the kestrel. Now — based just on those words — draw your impression of each bird — and color your drawing in. Now look at the illustrations in the book. How close did you come in really listening to the description?

FAMILY LIFE

There is one very unusual thing about the nesting habits of falcons. The female begins *incubating* her eggs (sitting on them almost full time to keep them warm) as soon as the first egg is laid, whereas most other birds wait until all their eggs are laid before starting incubation.

This means that the eggs hatch a day or two apart, instead of all at once. The first ones to hatch become, of course, older and larger, and the parents continue to feed them first. This means that when food is scarce, the younger, smaller ones starve.

This may seem cruel, but it's nature's way of making sure that at least one or two of the young will live in years when the supply of food is very limited.

After the eggs hatch — two to four for the peregrine and four or five for the kestrel — both parents are kept busy feeding themselves and the nestlings. The male kestrel even brings food to the female while she is sitting on her eggs and then brings food to the young after they hatch.

A peregrine in a power dive may reach speeds of 160 miles an hour or more — perhaps even as much as 180 miles an hour. That's faster than some small airplanes fly! Just as amazing, the peregrine has such great flying ability that it can pull out of this power dive with ease.

How fast is that?: Find out how fast some of the following go, and compare their speed to the peregrine's.

★ A baseball thrown by a pitcher like Nolan Ryan.

★ An automobile travelling at the speed limit on an interstate highway.

★ A hockey puck hit by someone like Wayne Gretzky.

★ A small, propeller-driven airplane.

★ A mallard duck flying at top speed.

Does this give you some idea how fast a peregrine can travel?

Feathered Fighter Planes

Most birds of prey — hawks and owls — catch their food with their strong, sharp claws or *talons*. The peregrine, however, captures its larger prey, such as ducks and pigeons, in a different and spectacular way. First the peregrine flies high above its target. Then, with powerful wing beats, it goes into a very fast dive. It may even fold its wings during the dive and drop like a stone!

Moving at tremendous speed, the peregrine strikes its prey with its feet clenched into a fist. The force of this blow stuns the target bird and sends it tumbling — and the peregrine then seizes the falling bird in its talons before it hits the ground. Is it any wonder that so many people admire falcons — and especially peregrines — for their flying ability?

HOME SWEET HOME

Some birds, such as the ovenbird and Baltimore oriole, weave beautiful nests which take a long time to build. Not these two falcons, though. The peregrine nests on cliff ledges, called an *eyrie* or *aerie* (both pronounced either AIR-ie or IR-ie); in cities, it nests on window sills and ledges high up on skyscrapers. There it simply lays its eggs without building any real nest at all. Many peregrines like cities. They seem to think a skyscraper is just another kind of cliff, and of course those city pigeons make great eating!

Kestrels nest in cavities in trees (or in nesting boxes built by humans), but, like the peregrines, they don't line it or build any sort of nest. They just lay their eggs at the bottom of the cavity or box.

Build a kestrel nesting box: You can get plans for one from a booklet called *Woodworking for Wildlife*. Write to the Pennsylvania Game Commission, Dept. MS, 2001 Elmerton Avenue, Harrisburg, PA 17120. The cost is $3.00 (plus a 6% tax for Pennsylvania residents). This book will tell you how to build nesting boxes for many birds and mammals, and it will also tell you how to place them for best results.

Nature's Helicopter --

You already know that the peregrine catches its prey by diving on it at high speed. Most falcons, even if they don't dive like the peregrine, seize their prey in the air, rather than on the ground. The little kestrel is an unusual and very different falcon, though.

From its perch on a wire or branch, the kestrel swoops down to grab insects and mice on the ground — but it does a lot more than that! Have you ever watched a helicopter hover in one spot without moving, and suddenly fly swiftly away? Well, that's exactly the sort of thing that this amazing little falcon does. When it's trying to locate its prey exactly, the kestrel will hover in mid-air only a few feet above the ground, wings fluttering rapidly, just like the rotors of a tiny helicopter. Sometimes it will hover like this in one spot for two or three minutes while it looks for a grasshopper, cricket, or mouse. There are few more interesting or beautiful sights in the bird world than a hovering kestrel!

Making a Comeback

Thanks to dedicated scientists working under the *Endangered Species Act* — a law to help save endangered species from extinction — the peregrine is coming back. Although these wonderful birds still have a long way to go, we can now hope that in a few years they'll be as abundant as they once were.

There are now at least 120 nesting pairs of peregrines in the United States east of the Mississippi River — probably more than 500 peregrines, counting young birds that haven't yet mated. West of the Mississippi, there are perhaps 3,000 peregrines, and there are many thousands in Canada and Alaska. This great bird is making a wonderful comeback.

A rare treat: Find out if there are any peregrine nesting sites near you. If there is one, try to see it from a distance. Don't go too close, though. Except in cities, nesting peregrines are easily disturbed; too much human activity may make them abandon their nest.

Environmentally Yours

★

In the 1950s and 1960s, an *insecticide* — a chemical used to kill insects — called *DDT* was widely used. DDT lasts a very long time in the soil and water, so that some creatures that weren't killed by it ate the DDT with their food. Then, larger creatures ate the small creatures, and they were then eaten by still larger creatures — all the way up to the large predators. This is what biologists call a *food chain*. The only problem was that the food chain became contaminated.

At each step up the food chain, the larger creature took in more and more DDT from its food, because it basically ate ALL the DDT that each of the preceding animals on the chain had eaten. The peregrines, at the top of the food chain, took in so much DDT that they began laying eggs with shells so thin they broke before hatching.

By the time the use of DDT was stopped in North America, peregrines were in danger of extinction. There were NO nesting peregrines left east of the Mississippi River in the United States, and only a few in the western United States. Those in northern Canada and Alaska were less affected, but even their numbers had dropped a great deal.

★

APPENDIX

SALT DOUGH RECIPE

Ingredients:

3 cups flour (any kind except self-rising)

1¼ cups warm tap water

1 cup salt

Materials:

Measuring cup, bowl, and spoon

Wooden board or piece of waxed paper taped to the table

Rolling pin (or the side of a smooth glass)

Plastic knife

1. Pour 1 cup of salt into a bowl.
2. Add 1¼ cups warm tap water to the salt, stirring until the salt dissolves.
3. Add 3 cups of flour to this mixture. Stir.
4. Mix and knead the dough by working it with your hands, shaping and reshaping it, until it is smooth and firm. Form it into a ball.
5. Use the dough right away or store it in a covered container in the refrigerator for up to a week.

To bake:
1. Have a grown-up preheat the oven to 250°. **NEVER USE AN OVEN BY YOURSELF.**
2. Use a rolling pin or the side of a large glass to roll out the dough. Don't make it too thick or it won't bake all the way through. Make your shapes, and place on a cookie sheet.
3. Bake small projects about 45 minutes to 1 hour. Large projects will take about 2 hours. Have a grown-up check the dough once in a while.
4. When golden, use a potholder to remove from oven. Let cool before painting.

PAPIER-MACHE RECIPE

Ingredients:

½ cup flour

¾ cup water

Materials:

Measuring cup

Shallow bowl and spoon

Newspaper cut into 1"-wide strips

1. Pour ½ cup flour in a bowl.
2. Add ½ cup of the water and stir. Keep the leftover water in case the paste gets too thick. (The paste should be like whipping cream before it is whipped, not like thick pudding.)
3. Lay one strip of newspaper into the papier-mache mixture at a time. Hold it up with one hand and squeeze out the excess with two fingers of the other hand.
4. Place the strips over the form, one at a time. Repeat with other strips.
5. If you put more than one layer of papier-mache on your project be certain to dry completely between layers — usually overnight.
6. The papier-mache object must be completely dry before painting — usually overnight. Paint as soon as possible, since homemade paste becomes moldy quickly, unless painted.

INDEX

MORE KIDS CAN! BOOKS
from Williamson Publishing

To order additional copies of **The Kids' Wildlife Book**, please enclose $12.95 per copy plus $2.50 for shipping. Follow "To Order" instructions on the last page. Thank you.

Over 250,000 copies sold!
THE KIDS' NATURE BOOK:
365 Indoor/Outdoor Activities and Experiences
by Susan Milord

Winner of the Parents' Choice Gold Award for learning and doing books, *The Kids' Nature Book* is loved by children, grandparents, and friends alike. Simple projects and activities emphasize fun while quietly reinforcing the wonder of the world we all share. Packed with facts and fun!

160 pages, 11 x 8½, 425 illustrations
Quality paperback, $12.95

ECOART!
Earth-Friendly Art & Craft Experiences for 3- to 9-year-olds
by Laurie Carlson

What better way to learn to love and care for the Earth than through creative art play! Laurie Carlson's latest book is packed with 150 projects using only recyclable, reusable, or nature's own found art materials. These fabulous activities are sure to please any child!

160 pages, 11 x 8½, 400 illustrations
Quality paperback, $12.95

THE KIDS' MULTICULTURAL ART BOOK
Art & Craft Experiences from Around the World
by Alexandra M. Terzian

Winner of the Parents' Choice Gold Award! Children will reach across continents and oceans with paper, paste, and paints, while absorbing basic sensibilities about the wondrous cultures of others. Children will learn by making such things as the *Korhogo Mud Cloth* and the *Wodaabe Mirror Pouch* from Africa, the *Chippewa Dream Catcher* of the American Indian, the *Kokeshi Doll* of Japan, *Chinese Egg Painting*, the Mexican *Folk Art Tree of Life*, the *Twirling Palm Puppet* from India, and the Guatemalan *Green Toad Bank*. A virtual feast of multicultural art and craft experiences!

160 pages, 11 x 8½, over 400 how-to-do-it illustrations
Quality paperback, $12.95

KIDS COOK!
Fabulous Food for the Whole Family
by Sarah Williamson and Zachary Williamson

Here's a cookbook written for kids by two teenagers who know what kids like to eat! *Kids Cook!* is filled with over 150 recipes for great tasting foods that kids ages 8 and up can cook for themselves and for their families and friends, too. Try breakfast bonanzas like *Breakfast Sundaes*, great lunches including *Chicken Shirt Pocket*, super salads like *A Whale of a Fruit Salad*, quick snacks and easy extras like *Nacho Nibbles*, delicious dinners including *Pizza Originale*, and dynamite desserts and soda fountain treats including *Chocolate Surprise Cupcakes*. All recipes are for "real," healthy foods — not cutesy recipes that are no fun to eat. Plus Nutri Notes, Safety First, and plenty of special menus for Father's Day, Grandma's Teatime, picnics, and parties. One terrific book!

176 pages, 11 x 8½, Over 150 recipes, illustrations
Quality paperback, $12.95

HANDS AROUND THE WORLD
365 Creative Ways to Build Cultural Awareness & Global Respect
by Susan Milord

The latest book by award-winning author Susan Milord invites children to experience, taste, and embrace the daily lives of children from the far corners of the earth. In 365 days of experiences, it tears down stereotypes and replaces them with the fascinating realities of our differences and our similarities. Children everywhere can plant and grow, write and tell stories, draw and craft, cook and eat, sing and dance, look and explore, as they learn to live in an atmosphere of global respect and cultural awareness that is born of personal experience.

160 pages, 11 x 8½, over 400 illustrations
Quality paperback, $12.95

KIDS AND WEEKENDS!
Creative Ways to Make Special Days
by Avery Hart and Paul Mantell

Packed with truly creative ways to play, have fun, learn, grow, and build self-esteem and positive relationships, this book is a must for every parent, grandparent, babysitter and teacher. Hart and Mantell will inspire us all to transform some part of every weekend — even if it is only 30 minutes — into a special experience. Everything from backyard nature to putting on a magic show to creating a bird sanctuary to writing a book about yourself to environmentally-sound activities indoors and out. Whatever your interests, no matter how busy you are, kids and their families will savor special weekend moments.

176 pages, 11 x 8½, over 400 illustrations
Quality paperback, $12.95

Over 250,000 copies sold!

KIDS CREATE!
Art & Craft Experiences for 3- to 9-year-olds
by Laurie Carlson

What's the most important experience for children ages 3 to 9? Why, to create something by themselves. Carlson provides over 150 creative experiences ranging from making dinosaur sculptures to clay cactus gardens, from butterfly puppets to windsocks. Plenty of help for the parents working with the kids, too! A delightfully innovative book.

160 pages, 11 x 8½, over 400 illustrations
Quality paperback, $12.95

KIDS MAKE MUSIC!
Clapping and Tapping from Bach to Rock
by Avery Hart and Paul Mantell

No instruments necessary — just hands, feet, and wiggly bodies! Kids are natural music makers, and with the kid-loving music makers, Avery Hart and Paul Mantell, children everywhere will be doing the *Dinosaur Dance*, singing the *Dishwashin' Blues*, cleaning their rooms to *Rap*, belting it out in a *Jug Band* or An *Accidental Orchestra*, putting on a *Fairy Tale Opera*, learning to Tap Dance or creating a *Bona Fide Ballet* (homemade tutu included)! Those hands will be clapping, those feet will be tapping, those faces will be grinning, and they may be humming anything from Bach to Rock.

160 pages, 11 x 8½, with hundreds of illustrations
Quality paperback, $12.95

ADVENTURES IN ART:
Art & Craft Experiences for 7- to 14-year-olds
by Susan Milord

Imagine an art book that encourages children to explore, to experience, to touch and to see, to learn and to create . . . imagine a true adventure in art. Here's a book that teaches artisans' skills without stifling creativity. Covers making handmade papers, puppets, masks, paper seascapes, seed art, tin can lantern, berry ink, still life, silk screen, batiking, carving, and so much more. Perfect for the older child. Let the adventure begin!

160 pages, 11 x 8½, 500 illustrations
Quality paperback, $12.95

THE KIDS' BOOK OF CRAZY CONCOCTIONS
Mysterious Mixtures for Creative Fun
by Jill Frankel Hauser

Mix it, stretch it, knead it, squish, squash, mush, and mash — however it's done, kids are bound to have endless hours of fun and learning as they concoct the craziest things. Hauser inspires kids with artistic creations including a geo-pea sculpture, glitter snow, soap-on-a-rope, and body paint. Fun is the theme with lots of fun along the way!

160 pages, 11 x 8½, over 300 illustrations
Quality paperback, $12.95

TALES ALIVE!
Ten Multicultural Folk Tales with Art, Craft & Creative Experiences
by Susan Milord

Award-winning author, Susan Milord brings ten folk tales from around the world to life with a myriad of exciting, relevant hands-on activities. *Tales Alive!* will lock these universal stories into the hearts and minds of children for many years to follow. Includes wondrous stories from Native America, Australia, Italy, Argentina, China, and Russia, and many other countries. A virtual feast of fun!

160 pages, 8½ x 11, full-color illustrations
Quality paperback, $14.95

To Order:

At your bookstore or order directly from Williamson Publishing. We accept Visa and MasterCard (please include number and expiration date), or send check to:

Williamson Publishing Company
Church Hill Road, P.O. Box 185
Charlotte, Vermont 05445

Toll-Free phone orders with credit cards: **1-800-234-8791**

Please add $2.50 for postage per total order. Satisfaction is guaranteed or full refund without questions or quibbles.

Prices may be higher when purchased in Canada.

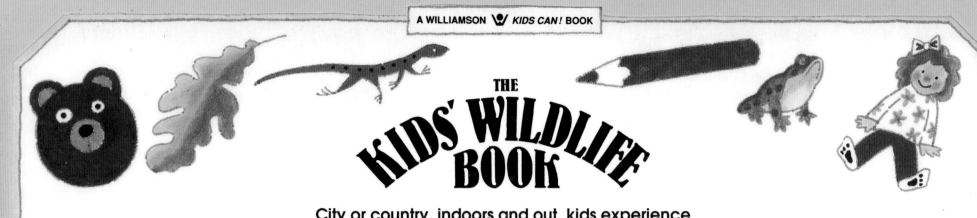

THE KIDS' WILDLIFE BOOK

City or country, indoors and out, kids experience the remarkable worlds of wild creatures.

Introduce children to the wildlife of North America, from toads to timber wolves, from bats to bobcats, from owls to armadillos. *The Kids' Wildlife Book* provides fascinating insights, remarkable experiences, and unforgettable anecdotes that dispel myths, encourage understanding, and delight children of all ages.

Over 100 learning experiences use science, language arts, nature, math, art, and crafts to explore animal lives and their natural habitats:

- ★ **Walk like a lynx with homemade snowshoes**
- ★ **Experiment with oil and water to learn how beavers keep dry**
- ★ **Try to catch a fish heron-style**
- ★ **Read Native American legends to gain understanding**
- ★ **Compare your heartbeat to a hibernating bear's**
- ★ **Create a moose with palm print antlers**

With the turn of every page, author Warner Shedd's thoughtful approach fills children with wonder and respect for the creatures with whom they share this planet.

"What a delightful, information-filled book to give to my grandchildren, and, I am quick to add, there are many facts that I did not know within its pages." **— Will Curtis, *The Nature of Things***

For children ages 4 to 10 — and their families!

WARNER SHEDD was a regional executive for the National Wildlife Federation for 20 years and has written extensively about wildlife.

WARNER SHEDD

WILLIAMSON PUBLISHING CHARLOTTE, VERMONT 05445

ISBN 0-913589-77-2

$12.95 U.S.

cover design TREZZO-BRAREN STUDIO